ANGI

To:- Tess.

Best Wishes

Eddie & Mary

Powell

14/3/96.

ANGEL
IN WHITE BOOTS

by
Eddie Powell

West Runton:
Published by the author

To Mary
without whose steadfast love and devotion
there would have been no story to write

Also dedicated to Paul
who all through his life
loved and supported Angi

ISBN 0 9522271 0 X

First published in 1993 by Eddie Powell, Corner Cottage,
Water Lane, West Runton, Cromer, Norfolk NR27 9QP
Designed and typeset by Watermark, Hamilton Road, Cromer
Printed by Rounce & Wortley, North Walsham

CONTENTS

ILLUSTRATIONS

CHAPTER 1

GOOD NEWS, BAD NEWS

The clatter of the alarm clock split the peace of my dreamless sleep. I looked with bleary eyes at the hands. Six a.m.! As my thoughts returned, I realised I was in bed alone. Of course. Mary was in hospital. She had been taken in the day before, and we were now expecting the birth of our second child. We had already been blessed with a son, five years before, and Paul was now in the temporary care of Mary's mum, who lived some two miles away. I went through my morning wash and shave with more than usual haste, quickly becoming more attuned to the awakening world. I had to get to a phone. The nearest was at the end of the block – this was 1960 and the age of a telephone in every house had not yet arrived.

My mind went back to the events of the previous day. Mary's father had taken her to the Loveday Street Hospital in the heart of the city of Birmingham, where she was going to be "started off" in labour at 2 p.m. Her labour started properly at about 6.30 p.m. but when I left her the nurse said I was to ring in the morning. (Dads generally didn't stay for the birth in the 1960s.)

In the phone box I was soon talking to the sister-in-charge of the ward. Mary had given birth at 2 a.m. to a daughter, birth weight six pounds thirteen ounces. I was relieved that this was within the normal range because Mary had been advised to go into this specialist maternity hospital since the baby was in the "breech" position. The nurse also told me that there had been no unusual or unexpected difficulty in the delivery, and that both mother and daughter were well.

The school at which I worked as a teacher was several miles from our house. The journey involved a walk of about a mile, and after that a twenty minute bus ride. As I walked kept on thinking, "We've done it at last. We've got our own Angela."

For five years we had wanted another baby, but in spite of all the tests available Mary had been unable to conceive. This was in sharp contrast to our experience with Paul, who must have been conceived shortly after our marriage because he was born in October 1955 just ten months after our wedding. All avenues had been explored. and one doctor even suggested that the reason for the lack of fertility was that Mary was too anxious. Anyway, now all the waiting was over. We could settle down to being a two-child family. We had chosen the baby's name a long time before on a visit to my home town in Gwent. In the little café/shop we heard an Italian woman calling her little girl by the name Angela, and we decided this would be a lovely name if we had a daughter.

On arrival at Halesbury School I was greeted with cries of, "Has anything happened yet?"

Halesbury is a special school for children with learning difficulties, situated between Oldbury and Halesowen. The headmaster, Norman Moore, and I had become acquainted when we had attended an evening course, and when a vacancy occurred at his school he asked me to apply. The school was very new and thus very unlike the two previous establishments at which I had worked. The staff were very friendly, and had taken a great interest in the progress of Mary's pregnancy.

When I visited Mary that night I found her radiant. She was sitting in bed eating a grape and she looked in great shape. We spent the time discussing matters concerning home and the new baby and soon the bell rang indicating visiting time was over. I was about to leave when Mary said, "Look, before you see Angela, there's something I think I should tell you."

This seemed fairly ominous, so I sat on the edge on the bed. The rest of the news was not long coming.

"One of the doctors has told me that the baby's left foot has a slight deformity. It is clubbed, but they are sure they can put it right with a simple operation."

"Well, that's all right then. Anyway, it's obviously not something to worry about, so you just concentrate on getting out of here quickly. Don't concern yourself too much about her foot: doctors can do wonderful things these days and I'm sure they'll soon put it right," I said, as always the optimist.

On the way out, I was permitted a glance at our baby – through a glass partition. This was the way all new fathers were treated by the hospital authorities in those days. As I gazed adoringly at the only part of her that was not covered by clothes, her face, she seemed to me to be so perfect that I couldn't really believe that there was anything at all wrong with her.

I slept well that night, secure in the knowledge that now that I had actually seen her, the simple operation suggested would quickly put everything right.

School next morning was fun. There were only a few days to go to the May half term break, and staff and children alike were in high spirits. And I, of course, had a special reason for these. I recounted to all who were interested the entire happenings of the previous evening. During the morning tea break Mrs Bragger, the school nurse, took me aside and said, "Look, Eddie, I think you should leave school now, go to the hospital and insist on seeing the doctors in charge of Mary and the baby."

"I don't think there is any need for that," I replied. "After all, the doctor assured Mary that there is nothing much wrong, and I don't want to go and make a fuss about nothing. Besides, I can't just go off and leave my class; who'll look after them?"

"Don't worry about that at all, I'll explain the whole situation to Mr Moore and he'll make the necessary arrangements. So, go this minute, and when you get to the hospital, see the doctor. If they try to put you off, stay there until you see him. Be prepared to wait, but get a full explanation of the baby's problems before you leave the hospital."

Mrs Bragger had been a sister at several hospitals and this, coupled with the fact that she was older than I, persuaded me that I ought to adopt this course. Without even consulting the headmaster, I ran out of the school to the bus stop. While I waited, I considered the irresponsibility of my action. Here was I, a teacher in the early years of what I hoped would be a successful career, leaving my class, without even consulting the head. A great reference I could expect from Norman Moore when the time came for me to apply for promotion!

The journey to Birmingham took about forty minutes. From the upper deck of the bus I looked down upon the hundreds of houses, and I wondered what troubles were worrying the occupants. The nearer I got to the hospital, the more anxious I became. Questions came to my mind. Why had the nurse at school seemed so concerned? Was there anything really to worry about? Suddenly, I didn't fancy going to the hospital one little bit.

As I had anticipated, there was some difficulty in getting to see the doctor. But, after a wait of thirty minutes or so, a nurse ushered me along through a long corridor to a small, bare room at the end. A tall, thin, young doctor was already there. As my eyes took in the almost unfurnished office, I wondered briefly whether this was a special room set aside by the hospital authorities for communicating bad news. I thought I would be strong enough to stand any news, however bad, but nothing could prepare me for what was to come.

"Hello, Mr Powell. I am the doctor who is treating your wife and baby. I'm sorry to have to tell you that there are many physical problems with your daughter. She has what we commonly call a 'full house'."

"What do you mean?" I inquired. "I know that there's something wrong with one of her feet, but when I saw her last night there didn't seem to be much that could be the matter, she looked so pretty."

He looked down at an invisible spot on the floor, just in front of me.

"But," he continued, speaking more gently now, "because of all the clothing she had on you couldn't see what is wrong. Let me explain things as best as I can. First, her back has a terrible curvature. Then, as you know, she has a clubbed foot. She also may have a pretty bad case of hydrocephalus – water on the brain. This will probably prevent her from developing any degree of intellectual ability. And her back passage has no opening to the outside. Now, I'm sorry to have to have given you such bad news, but if there are any questions you would like to ask me, I shall do my best to answer them."

I could tell by the way he spoke that this was a well rehearsed speech. My mind was in a state of total confusion. My experience of physical handicap was limited to the rare sight of someone being pushed along in a wheelchair. After what seemed like a long time but could only have been a few seconds, I heard myself say, in a calm voice, betraying the turmoil that I felt, "Look, I don't know much about these problems. What will be the consequences for the baby?"

He hesitated and cleared his throat as is he was playing for time. It seemed to me that he might be waiting for some inspiration to hit him. I could tell from the worried look on his face that he was desperately searching to find words to break the bad news. I wondered if he had ever done anything like this before. However, he seemed to collect his thoughts and explained.

"Well, of course, at this early stage in her life we can't give too accurate a prognosis. But I feel that we will only be wrong in minor details. First, the good news. The back passage problem will be able to be corrected, if all the internal organs are sound. If this is the case, as we anticipate, all that has to be done is to make an opening to the outside. This will have to be done without delay, as all her waste products at present are coming through her vagina. But, as to the other problems, they are not going to be solved. I don't think she will ever sit up, let alone walk, and the hydrocephalus will make it impossible for her to attend any school – even a special one. Naturally, it may be that if she lives for any length of time, certain remedial measures may be possible, but these will only be of minimal benefit. Even with all the luck in the world, we can't give you a normal baby."

I felt as if my whole life had suddenly caved in. All the plans we had already made for the baby were not going to be fulfilled. In fact, it seemed doubtful that she would live for long. Both Mary and I knew next to nothing about abnormalities, and I felt we would be completely unable to cope. There was a short silence and the doctor spoke again.

"Your wife must be told as soon as possible. Who would you think is the best person to do this?"

"I think it will be best if you do it," I answered. "You will be less emotional than I would be. And in any case, if Mary wants other details you would be able to supply them. But, I would be grateful if you would tell her before visiting time tonight, so that when I next see her, she will have faced the situation. But look, as I see it, the baby has no chance at all of anything like a normal life, so couldn't you do something to end what is going to be a burdensome life for her and for all of us?"

It was obvious to him that I was not responsible for what I was saying, and he fixed me with a look and said, "I know something of what you are going through. But this sort of thing does happen, and you and your wife just will have to cope."

He looked hard at me again for a few seconds and then abruptly left the room.

Alone in the bareness of that room, I felt my body stiffen. My knees started to shake, but I knew that I had to get out of that awful room, and quickly. Using what little self-control I could muster I ran to the bus stop.

As it was well into the afternoon by now, I didn't go back to school for the rest of that day. I took the news to my inlaws, who were in as much confusion as I. They had two daughters, Mary and her sister who lived in America. Mary's dad owned a car and he offered to give me a lift into the hospital that night. I well remember his comment during the journey, "Perhaps it might be for the best if she didn't live."

He was not an unkind man, but it was clear that he, like me, had no idea of how to handle the situation. I asked him not to visit Mary on this occasion. I thought she and I would be so upset, now that we both knew the score, and I didn't want anyone to intrude on our private hell. I couldn't even begin to consider his feelings – I was too consumed with the misery of wondering how Mary was reacting. I walked at a snail's pace up the sanitised-smelling corridors, dread marking every step. I don't know how I made those last few steps into the ward.

I peered into the crowded ward and was amazed to see Mary

sitting up in bed, looking positively radiant. Well, I thought, at least she's taking it a lot better than I did. Maybe she's that much stronger than I. When I got close enough she gave me the biggest hug I'd ever had! She began to chatter in a most happy way. I thought, "She hasn't grasped what the doctor told her. She's so thrilled with the baby that she hasn't understood the implications of all the handicaps. How can she be so cheerful when we've got so much to worry about?"

As the chatter showed no sign of getting at all serious it gradually dawned on me that Mary had no idea of the news that the doctor had imparted to me earlier. But by now I had given so many hints to her that there was much she didn't know, that I heard myself say, "You mean to say the doctor hasn't told you anything about Angela's medical problems?"

She looked mystified.

"What do you mean? The doctor hasn't been to see me at all today."

There was no escape for me. I would have to tell her myself here and now. I braced myself for the ordeal.

With as much detail as I could remember, I told her.

She began to cry. Not very loudly, but with quiet, short sobs. She was hurting so much in the deepest parts of her being. I cried too, but all the time trying to hide it from her. How much easier for both of us, I thought, if she had been told by the doctor. When we had both somewhat regained our poise, I looked around and noticed that several of the other mothers were crying for us too.

Just before visiting time was over, a nurse asked Mary if she would like to feed the baby. Mary said through her still tear-filled eyes, "No, I don't think I could at the moment."

I was astonished at this remark. Mary was so fond of her baby that I couldn't have expected such a statement, not in a million years. But as the nurse left her bedside, Mary called her back, urgently, "Yes, please. Please bring her to me."

I can honestly say this was the only occasion that Mary re-jected Angela – and this rejection lasted all of five seconds.

It seemed that a lot of the tension had now gone out of the business, at least as far as I was concerned. Mary knew, and I realised that much of the worry was due to the fact that I was trying to think of a way in which I could somehow lessen the burden for Mary, but the situation had seemed impossible. However, now that things were more or less out in the open, it looked a little less hopeless. We both found out in later years that once a difficulty is acknowledged and faced, its terror is always diminished. Anyway, for whatever reason, when I left the hospital that night, I felt a little more at ease in the situation.

In the course of hospital visiting, it is often the unofficial, casual dialogues with members of staff that turn out to be more useful than the more formal interviews. Such was the case on the next visit.

We had become quite friendly with a number of the nursing staff, but one, of obvious Irish descent, had become one of our favourites. She was so kind and understanding, and had that kind of middle aged, sympathetic, open sort of face, that was very reassuring to a young, inexperienced couple such as Mary and I. As we had our usual natter, she said, "You know, if I were you, I'd leave her here for us to look after. She's going to be a terrible problem for you to be able to look after at home. But here we have all the facilities to care for her properly, and to make her short life as comfortable as possible. And you can always try for another child; you're young enough still."

"But surely there must be things that can be done, operations performed, medicines given," blurted Mary, in disbelief.

From the look on her face I could tell that she, like myself, could no longer contemplate the course of action that the nurse had proposed. We had been married for only five years, but already there was a kind of telepathy between us.

"Well, you heard what the doctor said, and I think it would be wise for you to take notice of that and what I am advising you now. If you take your baby home, you'll have a terrible time. It'll be a twenty-four hour a day job, and you won't be able to give your son the attention he needs. No, your best plan would be to go home and forget you ever had her. But the decision has got to be yours. After all she is your baby, not mine.

I have to go now, but do think over what I have said."

We did – for about five seconds after she left. I was the first to speak.

"There's no way we can do what she advised. But we must be sure of one thing. If we take her home, we must be prepared to devote our entire lives to her. Everything, and that includes Paul, will have to take second place. If you and I agree with this, then we'll take her home as soon as they allow us, and as soon as you're fit again."

Mary's face was not so unhappy now.

"That's what I want to do. We'll manage somehow," she whispered.

Whilst Mary completed her obligatory ten days in the hospital, nothing much happened. We gradually got used to the fact that Angela, in spite of her special needs, needed just about the same kind of attention that any other baby would demand.

Mary was convinced by now, that if she could take our baby home, and take her for a walk in the new pram we had bought for her, all would be well – we would cope.

Paul had not been able to see Mary or the baby for ten days (children were not permitted to visit). So on the day of the homecoming I took him with me. He was not allowed in to the hospital but Mary brought Angela to the window for him to see. He looked at her and said ,"I like your baby, Mum". This was the start of a very special relationship between Paul and his little sister.

The homecoming itself was not without humour. An ambulance brought my two ladies home, and I proudly carried Angela in. The ambulance men carried Mary on a stretcher and laughingly dumped her in the front garden pretending that they would not carry her any further. It was a lovely, sunny day and a number of our neighbours were out on their doorsteps, enjoying all the good-humoured banter going on between Mary and the two ambulancemen.

CHAPTER 2

OPERATIONS

The period of home life with Mary, Paul and Angela all together did not last long. Routine at home was reasonably normal. I had a few days off work because of the Whitsun half term holiday, and on the second day of the break, Mary was almost overwhelmed by the arrival of a beautiful bouquet of flowers, bearing the message, "from the staff at Halesbury". It was a small but potent reminder that people were thinking about us. Years later a similar gift from another staff gave us some comfort when it was most needed.

However, we had to face up to the fact that Angela had to enter hospital again very shortly. Something had to be done about the back passage problem. So, after four days, Mary and I found ourselves in a waiting room at the Birmingham Children's Hospital. We had been informed that we would be seen by a certain Mr Gourevitch. We were quite apprehensive about being dealt with by someone with a foreign sounding name – perhaps this was an indication of our low morale. But our fears were quickly allayed by the man's charming and efficient manner.

His assessment was that all the essential parts of the bowels and other internal organs were probably undamaged, but without an operation no-one could be sure. But if this were so, all that would be required would be to make an opening on the outside, and possibly some re-alignment of the inside parts. Accordingly, arrangements were made to admit Angela in ten days' time. Again we had a short respite at home. Again doubts and fears for the future began to dominate our thinking.

The next ten days seemed very lengthy. We didn't want to be parted from our baby, but we did want to get the operation over and done with, and for it to be a success. This anxious period was one of many we were to experience.

On the day of Angela's admission, the huge waiting room was filled with parents and children. The cries of the little ones mingled with the sharp scolds of the parents. It was rather like a kindly, tolerant bedlam. The children had apparently all kinds of diseases and difficulties. Here, one almost completely covered with bandages. Over there, one with nothing obviously wrong. And in the midst of all this, we had our Angela, a small pink bundle wrapped in white.

It was here that we found our first example of the thoughtlessness and lack of tact in people. Most people in our experience are most willing to help. The number of people with physical handicap is so small that most people are at a loss to know how to react when confronted by it. It is also clear that thirty years ago public awareness and sympathy was limited. Thanks to the efforts of the various governments, and the endeavours of the voluntary societies, there is much more understanding of both mental and physical handicaps now. Also when a "normal" person meets someone with a handicap, it is often the "normal" one who suffers embarrassment.

Our first experience of this kind was like this. Mary and I were waiting for the admission procedure to be completed, when Mary entered into conversation with a middle-aged woman who was the grandmother of a child who was in the hospital for a tonsillectomy. Naturally, the exchange turned to, "And what's wrong with your baby?" By this time, Mary could talk about Angela without bursting into tears. After listening for a while, the woman observed, "Well, I think in cases like this it would have been better if the children died at birth."

Mary and I were stunned. My wife, who had already worked herself into a state of extreme anxiety near to hysteria, clasped her precious bundle a little closer to her bosom, and with what appeared to me remarkable self-control answered, "We don't think so."

At length, we gave up our baby to the temporary care of the hospital authorities. Everything seemed to be under control, and although the operation struck us as being extremely dangerous, we were put at ease by Mr Gourevitch's Central

European self-confident manner Mary had decided to breastfeed Angela, and so before we left a nurse had to show her how to express quantities of milk. This was then kept in little containers which we took each day.

Three days later the operation was performed and to our relief it was successful. We were, of course, delighted but behind our optimism there was always the question, "What will go wrong next?" We knew that a certain degree of anxiety would never leave us.

Before Angela could be discharged, Mary had to have a period of instruction. On each evening visit she would ask the same question, "When can Angela come home?"

At last Mr Gourevitch succumbed to Mary's persistence, and gave an affirmative, if somewhat conditional, answer to Mary's question. Angela could be taken home if Mary would be able to manage the post-operative treatment, which consisted of keeping the anus open. This was achieved by putting on a surgical glove and inserting a finger. This had to be done several times a day. Because Angela's discharge depended upon Mary's ability to learn how to do this, she proved to be a very quick learner. Instruction was given by a nursing sister, with me being present. I thought this was a wise precaution in case Mary was not able to do it for any reason. At one of these "training sessions" we were astounded when the sister said, "You know, you'd be well advised to leave her with us. She's going to need a lot of attention which will take up a lot of your time. And besides, we have all the facilities to cope with any emergencies which will probably occur."

We recalled similar advice from another nurse in a different place, and Mary told her quite firmly that we were perfectly capable of caring for our baby. In our own minds we never had any doubt that this was true, and that we were doing the right thing by taking Angela home. We firmly believed that we could care for our baby by instinct, and if this failed love would fill the gap.

Life at home progressed quietly. Paul was doing quite well at the local infants' school which was situated across the road from our house, and he loved Mary pushing Angela over the road to meet him from school. There was a very special relationship between them growing. We did our best not to neglect him in any way, but inevitably our thoughts were focussed on Angela and her difficulties. The next one of them to be tackled was the matter of the clubbed foot. This required the attention of a Mr Allen, an orthopaedic surgeon at the hospital. In due course, Angela was operated upon and in due course was returned home, complete with a plaster on her leg which looked far too cumbersome for her small body. It made her very heavy to lift, and necessitated father's help to hold her leg out of the water at bath time. After two weeks the plaster had to be taken off because her toes were turning blue. We decided not to have the plaster put on again in view of the complications which it seemed to involve.

Mary and I learned many things during the first few weeks of Angela's life. We were told some old wives' tales. Mary's grandmother, a very kindly old lady, expressed the opinion that the baby's foot and leg might be strengthened by thrice daily rubbing with "neat's foot oil". (I had no idea at the time what a "neat" was, but I have found out since that it is an old name for a deer.) Because we were desperate to do anything at all, no matter how bizarre, to help, I took it upon myself to undertake this duty. I lost count of the number of hours I spent with this oil on my hands, systematically working up and down the leg with great vigour. Nothing was gained, but we were glad to have even the flimsiest of straws to clutch at.

Generally, we found people not to be very helpful. Friends and acquaintances were not unkind, but they were just unable to understand our emotions. Nevertheless, there was a great deal of goodwill shown towards us and one small act touched us deeply. Mary and I took Paul and Angela shopping in Dudley, which was the nearest town to where we lived. We went into Woolworth's and whilst we were browsing a lady whom we had never seen before came up to us. (Many people, unknown to us, knew Angela had "something wrong".)

"I'm so sorry to hear about your little girl," she said. "I would love to buy something for her."

She took us to the toy counter, and bought a cuddly Dopey, one of the seven dwarfs. He was very colourful, and covered in a furry material. We thanked her and went home. Dopey became a big part of Angela's life. He always went everywhere with her. When she went into hospital he went too, and during the following months Angela pulled all the furry material off him (this was whilst she was so ill). So many of our friends at different times knitted outfits for Dopey as gifts for her. Angela and Dopey were quite inseparable.

The next year was punctuated with regular and frequent visits to the Birmingham Children's Hospital for check-ups. These followed a pattern: a tedious journey followed by a long wait in a crowded foyer, and finally a short interview with either Mr Allen or Mr Gourevitch which invariably ended with the comment, "Everything that can be done is being done. Apart from keeping an eye on her general health we can do nothing more."

We couldn't accept that her condition was beyond improvement, and we knew that we would explore every avenue, no matter how unlikely, if there was any chance that somehow, somewhere, sometime, something could be done to help Angela to be able to live as normal a life as possible.

The numerous hospital visits continued. Mary and I found these, although routine, exhausting. There was always the uncertainty that something would be found wrong with Angela's kidneys, bladder or in any one of a number of possible weak spots. And the prospect of any hospital visit soon became quite depressing in itself.

Such was the pattern of our lives for a year or so. Then quite out of the blue, and much to our surprise and delight, Mr Allen suggested that an attempt might be made to straighten the curvature of her spine. I had looked at Angela's back on many occasions, and indeed it was a terrible sight. But the surgeon's idea had given us new hope that this was the first of a series of treatments that would dramatically improve the quality of our little one's life. He went on to explain that the bottom few pairs of ribs were fused, making the spine impossible to straighten. If the ribs were cut away, then the curvature might be corrected. It would involve an extensive operation, followed by a long period in plaster. We were assured that there would be no risk in the procedure, and there was every chance of success.

It was during this interview that we first heard the term "spina bifida". It seems incredible now that Angela had lived for two years without anyone telling us the name of the main handicap she was suffering from. Mr Allen explained that it meant "divided spine", and that the spinal cord protruded – in many cases it came right outside the body, but Angela's was lying just under the skin.

Until this conversation had taken place, we had been given little hope that any remedial measures for Angela's problems might be taken. At home, she had been a contented baby, but of course the familiar milestones of normal development were not all present. So we could not boast about her being able to sit up, crawl, or toddle, but she had begun to speak a little.

So, over the next few weeks, arrangements were made for her to be admitted to the usual hospital once again. First she had to see the surgeon, who was disappointed to find that a sac of cerebro-spinal fluid had collected at the point of curvature, and the proposed corrective treatment of the spine could not be carried out until the sac had first been removed. We all had to face the trauma of a small operation before the more difficult one.

At this time we were quite involved with the local churches. Mary's father had been a full time minister, but he had given it up and he now found himself employed at a factory in Oldbury. He still took services on a freelance basis, and in fact he usually occupied two or three different pulpits each week. On a few occasions he had roped me in to read the lessons, or assist in some other way. He was a firm believer in healing through prayer and the laying on of hands, as described many times in the New Testament.

An itinerant evangelist, Peter Scothern, was holding a series of meetings at the Midland Institute, in the centre of Birmingham. Peter was then at the beginning of what was to become a world wide ministry of healing and preaching. Mary and her father seemed keen to take Angela to one of the meetings, so a few nights later we were gathered with a couple of hundred people in a large room. Although not fully convinced of the wisdom of all this, I felt an air of expectancy. As I looked around I could see that many were obviously very sick indeed. Most were middle aged women. After the usual hymns, choruses and so on, Peter preached a very powerful sermon. Then he invited those who were in poor health and wanted to be prayed for to make their way to the front. Perhaps twenty people took the opportunity, and each one was individually prayed for. Some were thrown to the ground by the power of the Spirit. This manifestation of God's power was new and strange to me then, but in the years to come I was to witness it on many occasions.

As the meeting progressed, some claimed instantaneous healing of incurable diseases. Angela was prayed for without any apparent change in her condition: her left leg still had little strength or movement, and her back was still as curved as ever.

On our next visit to the hospital, it was found that on examination, the sac of fluid had gone. We were absolutely amazed and gave God thanks for answered prayer. This was not the only time we witnessed answers to prayers, but the mystery remains as to why Angela was never completely healed, despite the many times she was prayed for.

The surgeon, Mr Allen, was as perplexed as we were at the disappearance of the sac. He was not as inclined as we were to give God the credit, but neither could he offer any other reasonable explanation. However, the healing was effective, and the way was now clear for the operation to straighten Angela's spine.

We have heard of, read about and met people who when faced with such an adversity as ours have disclaimed belief in God. We never had such difficulties, and for all our married life Mary and I have had a very strong religious faith. Of course, from time to time we have asked the unanswerable question – why? But in the end we have come to the conclusion that it was all a matter of God's will. In any case, over the years, we have learned to count our blessings in regard to Angela's intellectual and personality development, and the vast amount of love and companionship she has brought into our lives.

CHAPTER 3

A VERY LUCKY GIRL

We still had not quite made up our minds finally about the operation. There were many questions still to be settled, and the chief one was, "Is there any possibility of further damage to the spinal cord?"

Angela had normal development in her right leg, and some in her left. Naturally, if work was done on her spine, there must be an element of risk that some of this movement might be lost. At least, this was the synopsis of the interviews we had had with several doctors. But we were much encouraged by the experience with Peter Scothern, and after a few days' thought, we informed the hospital that we wished to go ahead, although we still had some reservations.

Angela was admitted three days before the proposed date of the surgery. It was a coincidence that a near neighbour had a boy of seven who had to have a hole-in-the-heart operation in the same hospital on the same day that Angela was to have hers. So, James' parents and Mary and I were together in a waiting room whilst the two children were battling for their lives upstairs. The hours passed so slowly, and each time we heard footsteps in the corridor outside our hearts leaped with anticipation and fear, for none of us could be sure of the outcome.

James was "done" first, and the doctors were quite elated at their success. James' parents left to see their child, whilst we waited and waited.

After six hours we were not as alert as we might have been. Then the surgeon came into the room and told us the operation had been successful, and we could see our baby in half an hour. We were relieved of course, but still quite anxious. Still we managed to be outwardly calm, until we were led up to what I presumed was an intensive care ward. We couldn't recognise Angela amongst the other bandaged babies. The nurse guided us to her cot, and we were shocked to see her enclosed in plaster. This plaster extended from the top of her head right down to her toes. Only her face and right leg were left unplastered. She lay in an oxygen tent, helpless, pale and innocent. The thought came to me again and again, "What has she done to deserve all these problems?"

Mary reached through the small opening in the clear plastic and squeezed Angela's hand. Angela, more or less awake now, turned her eyes toward us and gently smiled.

Our daily visits became increasingly exciting. We longed to be able to comfort Angela with our arms, but all we could do was to touch her tiny hands through the hole in the oxygen tent.

A few evenings later whilst we sat there brooding, waiting, the sister told us that if we were gentle, Angela could be picked up. If we were gentle! Sister unzipped the plastic, and Mary picked up our daughter. What a strange feeling it was for me when Mary handed her over. It felt as if I was handling a large drainpipe. I gently rubbed the only part of her that was accessible, her right leg and face.

We were very pleased with the result of the operation. Not only was she appreciably taller, but her back was perfectly straight. We cried together, but this time the tears were of joy.

Day by day we visited, and gradually became aware that Angela seemed to be getting thinner and weaker. Not that we could see much of her, but her face showed that she wasn't as well as she had been. Five days later, Mary, who visited all day (I went in the evenings after school) telephoned me at school to tell me that something had gone drastically wrong and that the doctor had said that Angela had only a short time to live.

I was able to leave my class, and when I arrived at the ward, Mary greeted me with, "We're taking her home."

This was a surprise. I had been under the impression that after the operation Angela would need a great deal of specialised care which we could not provide at home. Mary quickly explained that she had seen the surgeon, who had informed her that, because of the way in which the plaster had been put on, Angela had been unable to feed properly, and this had caused her weakened condition. Mary had told him to take off the plaster – if Angela was going to die, she would do so at home.

Thus, once again, we removed our baby from the care of the hospital authorities. Under Mary's care at home, she did not die. Daily, we could sense the strength returning to that fragile body. But gradually, too, her back reverted to its former, twisted shape, and we felt a distressing sense of being let down. The agonies of the previous weeks had been for nothing. But at least, we still had our baby.

And, to everyone's astonished delight, Angela became stronger and healthier, as the influence of love's healing power began to take effect. Unhappily, she was in no way improved by the recent surgery. In fact, we suspected that the already weak left leg had lost a great deal of its already limited movement. Now, we felt really up against it. We had tried the experts, and they had proved powerless to help. We had no idea what we might do next. We even began to believe the prognosis that had been given soon after Angela's birth – that she would never walk or even sit up.

During this vital period of Angela's life, I did a one-year, full-time course at Birmingham University, and although I was at home in the evenings, it was often very late when I did get home, and then I had my "homework" to do. As a result of the course, I got a teaching post at a boarding school in the tiny village of Standon, near Eccleshall, in Staffordshire. So we sold our lovely little house and took up residence in one of the staff houses situated in the grounds of the school.

My job entailed much work during the evenings and at weekends, and I feel now some regret that I was not at home more to support Mary, Paul and Angela. However, as happens often in life, a seemingly chance event gave new hope. Mary was reading the daily paper a few months after Angela's last hospitalisation, when she drew my attention to a picture and article. This told of a young African boy who, because of a congenital back deformity, was able to make his way around only on all fours with a hopping action. In his native village he was called the "Grasshopper". A missionary had discovered his plight and was bringing him to England for treatment at the Orthopaedic Hospital, Oswestry. The surgeon, a Professor Roaf, was proposing to replace the defective parts of the little boy's spine with bullock bones. This seemed to us a most fantastic thing, and we both simultaneously spoke aloud the question, "If he can do something for this boy, can he do something for Angela?"

We were quick to show the article to our friends, who did not all share our enthusiasm. It was obvious that they didn't want to encourage us in a course of action that might raise our hopes, only to dash them later. The local doctor didn't feel able to support us in this matter, and he wouldn't give us a letter to give us access to Mr Roaf. Finally, we were so frustrated that Mary decided to write personally to him.

As she wrote, every letter on the page seemed to give her fresh hope. She looked up from time to time, and gave that certain flicker of a smile that only those who know they are doing the right thing can give.

My feelings were mainly those of doubt; was there any point in all this? All the doctors in Birmingham had indicated that nothing could be done, and so why could this man from Shropshire be able to more? Perhaps the "Grasshopper's" case was quite different from Angela's. I could see that if I thought too much about it, I might persuade Mary to give up her idea. I didn't want to do this, so when the letter was finished I ran to the local post box as quickly as I could. That letter carried with it all our hopes and prayers.

The reply came with almost obscene haste, and in a very short time we found ourselves knocking on yet another door – this time the door of the Oswestry Orthopaedic Hospital. We parked the car, a three year old Ford Popular, and made our way to the department we had been directed to attend. At the entrance we actually met, by chance, the "Grasshopper" with his female escort, and he was walking well, on two feet and with a straight back! This confirmed to us that not only were we were doing the correct thing, but that Angela would certainly be able to get some help here.

By now Angela was speaking well. She had lost some of her speech ability during her hospitalisation, but she had now more than made up for it. Furthermore, she took a great interest in speech as a means of self expression, and she was always eager to learn about and practise new words. Her vocabulary was quite large, so she was able to share in the agony and excitement of our Oswestry visit.

As we waited in a large room, filled with parents and children, our anxiety grew. The time went so slowly. Eventually, a tall, powerful, intense looking, middle aged man with a haversack on his shoulder appeared and began to look at various children, and to talk to their parents. Not for us the luxury of a consultation in a private office. Mary whispered, "That's him!"

I just could not believe that such an agricultural looking chap was in fact a world famous orthopaedic surgeon. But I was wrong. He was very courteous, in an old fashioned, gentlemanly way, and he talked to Angela and us at great length. Then after a very thorough examination of the little body, he told us that there was nothing he could do, and that Angela's problems were entirely different from those of the much publicised African boy. There could be no question of rebuilding her spine with bullock, or any other kind of bones. He concluded his remarks with, "But, if she is still alive in a year's time, bring her back and I will see if I can do anything then. She is too weak to consider any treatment now."

He moved on to another child, leaving three very disappointed people. Here was surely proof that my doubts had been justified. And a further cause for dread had been suggested to our minds – would she indeed be with us in twelve months' time? As we made our way towards the exit, we must have looked a picture of absolute dejection. But, in a firm act of defiance, Mary, with Angela clutched to her heart, strode determinedly to the car, with me a few steps behind. As we reached the car, she turned to face the hospital saying, "We'll be back."

The year passed without any major incident. It was with

hope and expectancy in our hearts that, once more, we set off for Oswestry to keep the appointment. Mary and I forced away our doubts with a constant chatter about everything under the sun, except the thing that was really on our minds. But this one thought kept us at least a little buoyant – Angela had lived for another year, she seemed to have gained in health and strength, and here we were, keeping the appointment.

Soon, we were confronted by the man in whom our hopes for our daughter were placed. He seemed mildly surprised that she had survived so well, and he made arrangements for her to be admitted as an in-patient as soon as possible. At home, each day, the postman was eagerly awaited, and often I would go out into the street to meet him. During this time our imagination and dreams all had the one vision – Angela, walking.

When the letter did finally arrive, it took us by surprise. We now had to face a new trial, that of separation. Angela had developed into very lovable child, and was beginning to talk very well. How would she cope with having to sleep apart from us? And, just as relevant, how would we cope with it? But for many months we had prayed hard for someone to be found who would be able to help her to walk, and this prayer would seem to be answered. It was a chance we just could not miss, no matter how difficult it might be for us.

Leaving her in the hospital, though, was a dreadful experience. We were distraught at leaving her, but we knew that there was no other way.

Oswestry is about forty miles from where we lived, and Mary made the journey every day for the next two months. Her normal practice was to leave home at about eight in the morning, stay with Angela all day, and return home about nine in the evening after putting Angela to bed. I accompanied her whenever I could, but this was only at alternate weekends, when I was not on school duty.

On one of our joint visits we couldn't find Angela in her usual place in the children's ward. At first, we thought that something had gone wrong, and that perhaps she was in one of the special wards. But she was in hospital only for calliper fitting, physiotherapy and so on. Soon, we located her in a side ward. When we asked the reason for the move, we were told that after Mary's last visit Angela had cried, upsetting the other children, so she had been put in this side ward with the door shut. The place terrified her, and Mary was quick to remonstrate with the ward sister. The matter was soon rectified, but Angela remembered the terror of it all, and occasionally spoke about it for many years afterward.

On another of our visits, we were asked to attend the fitting room, where we found Angela and a man from the local surgical appliance firm. He had to measure her for a full leg calliper and surgical boots. After fifteen minutes or so he asked, "And what about colour? Would you like black or brown?"

I saw the colour drain from Mary's face.

"I don't want either colour. She's going to have white ones. It's bad enough that she has to wear boots at all. Who ever heard of a little girl wearing black or brown boots? No, I want white for her."

He was taken aback. I guess he had not been at all prepared for Mary's verbal onslaught.

"But that's how it is. Under the National Health rules, black or brown are the only choices."

My wife returned to the attack.

"Well, I am not going to accept that. Why can't I have any colour I choose?"

"It's because black and brown are the most serviceable colours. Many parents would not look after their children's footwear properly, and a light colour would soon get to look very shabby if it were not cleaned regularly and well."

The fitter looked apologetic, almost as if he alone was responsible for the rules of the National Health Service. He spoke in a voice that suggested that he was making a deliberate effort to remain calm.

"Look, there is nothing I can do. But if you really are serious about white boots, there is only one way it can be done."

The sunshine returned to Mary's face.

"And how is that?"

"By paying for them yourself. Then you can have any colour you like."

"But how much will they cost?" she asked anxiously.

I shared and understood her worry. We were struggling financially and could hardly keep our heads above water.

"About sixteen pounds, I should think."

My heart sank. This was slightly more than one week's pay. Mary's face was taut, and I could sense the inner turmoil she was suffering. Without any further word, she gathered up Angela and swept out of the room and into the corridor. I gave the fitter a silent look of half apology and followed.

In the corridor Mary had stopped. As I prepared for tears, she said defiantly, "I just can't have her in those boots. Is there no way that we can afford the white ones?"

"Well, you know how tight the money is at present, but I expect we'll manage somehow. I tell you what, you go back in there and order the white boots."

She rushed back, and in no time at all we were walking out of the hospital, now in a more happy frame of mind. As we went, I heard Mary mutter to herself, "Who ever heard of a little girl in black boots?"

Four weeks later, we were all on our way to the surgical appliance firm's workshop in Walsall. As often as possible on the many trips we had to take with Angela, we included her brother. Right from the start I felt that, as he was part of the family, his part in Angela's struggle for some semblance of normality was to be a crucial one. As we waited rather impatiently, we began to wonder aloud what the new footwear would be like. Secretly, my worry was only, "What will Angela think of the boots?"

Very shortly we found out. I think we were all entranced by their sheer beauty. They were so small, like boots made for a doll. On they went, and they fitted perfectly. Of course, Angela couldn't actually walk on them yet, as she hadn't had any training, but it seemed to me that this was the beginning of a new era for us.

We were directed to the cashier's office. As we presented the bill together with the money it seemed like a very great amount of cash for such a small pair of boots. As she receipted the bill, she remarked casually, "You realise, of course that you could have had these for nothing on the National Health, if you had got the surgeon to indicate 'white' on the prescription?"

This looked like bureaucracy gone mad. It was the first and last time that we paid for Angela's white boots.

During the next few months, Mary and I experienced a wonderful sense of dedication in helping Angela in her first attempts to walk. A set of parallel bars had been provided by social services, and these were put up on a small patio at the back of the house. She used these, under our supervision, several times each day. It was a great joy to see her brother helping too.

One difficulty was overcome in a novel way. When she walked between the bars, I noticed that her left leg had a tendency to shoot out sideways. (We found out later that this was due to a congenital malformation of the hip.) An old pair of braces, long discarded in favour of a belt, was pressed into service. After a few trials, we managed to fix it so that the leg was held in place more or less facing front. This arrangement did not look very elegant, but it worked reasonably well.

Soon afterwards, it was her birthday. As the time for the celebration approached, we were all very conscious of a debt of gratitude to God for sparing her. In fact, as each later birthday came round, we would think of the number of times we had been told that she would not reach a certain age, or attain a particular stage of development. On her third birthday, we confidently expected that her life expectancy would be normal.

Amid all the presents, she suddenly broke off from her play, and remarked to me, "I think I'm a very lucky girl."

I agreed, presuming she was referring to her many gifts, but she continued, "Yes, because I have my parallel bars!"

I glanced at Mary and could see that she, too, was fighting hard to keep back the tears.

CHAPTER 4

HEADACHES

Mary and I began to feel increasingly isolated. We could cope quite well with the present problems, but the future of our daughter was always our most prominent concern. Most of the time we just could not visualise any future for her. In our more optimistic moments we pondered on the progress she had already made, and this occasionally provided us with some hope. But, in all truth, we could not imagine a life for her which was not in some sort of protected environment amongst other physically handicapped people.

We wanted to meet with other parents whose children were trying to cope with similar handicaps to Angela's. Mary wrote an article for the local paper describing the disability and inviting anyone interested to contact us. The result was that two or three couples met at our home at regular intervals and we shared our problems. This small beginning soon blossomed, and before long we were up to fifteen couples, and having to hire a hall to meet. Unknown to us, similar groups were springing up all over the country, and eventually they were amalgamated into a national Association for Spina Bifida and Hydrocephalus.

In the meantime, Angela was making slow progress with her walking practice. Two steps today, three the next and so on. Then, the whole length of the bars – all of two metres! The day this happened we could hardly have been more pleased than if she had run a marathon. In just over a year she graduated from the bars to a walking frame. And now she was approaching school age – which presented us with yet another problem.

I wish I knew then what I know now. (That would surely make a good song title.) I fancy that we all have thought this from time to time, but in regard to Angela's schooling it was indeed so true.

It seems to me now that the best place for any handicapped child of school age is at an "ordinary" school. Certainly, there would be problems, such as what would be done about physical education and games lessons. Also, the child might well need special help with feeding and toileting. Nowadays, special welfare assistants can be employed to take care of any handicapped child's special needs, but, in the sixties, special help of this kind was not so readily available, at least in ordinary schools. Unless a disabled child is to be forever condemned to a life of dependence and protected care, the sooner he faces up to the pressures of the normal world, the better. I feel I can speak with some authority on the subject, having been the head of a residential school for physically handicapped children, and the head of two primary schools.

Of course, much will depend on the attitude of the head and staff as to whether a child with handicaps is admitted to an ordinary school. But with goodwill on everyone's part, I have seen a number of these arrangements working well. In these cases, both the disabled child and the other children, and the school staffs, have benefitted from the experience. From the point of view of the local education authorities, it costs the ratepayers much less, even after allowing for the payment of welfare assistants.

Social services were a disappointment. Occasionally, we would be visited, but usually we were able to impart much more information than we received.

But, with the limited knowledge then at our disposal, we made local enquiries, and made an appointment to visit the nearest special school for physically handicapped children. This was the Blackfriars School, at Newcastle-under-Lyme, twelve miles from our home. I don't quite know what I expected it to be like, but I was surprised by the variety of the handicaps of the children, and the cheerfulness of staff and children alike. The building was quite new, and Mary, Angela and I were very impressed with the whole ambience of the place. We had no hesitation at all in accepting a place when it was offered by the headmaster, Mr Hollingshurst. Next, we had to think about transport arrangements. Mary was quite prepared to do this herself, but it was the Local Education Authority's responsibility, and they made a contract with a taxi firm. Mary took Angela for the first few days, while we all got used to the idea of our younger child going to school, but after that she was taken by a taxi, usually driven by a Mr Hubbard.

This gentleman came to play an important role in our lives. He was not merely someone who drove Angela to and from school, but a person who played a crucial part in her integration into school. For a number of years, she hadn't spent a single hour away from the comfort of the family, and for her to have to be parted from all of us for the best part of the day could have been agony for her. In helping her to overcome the pain of parting, Mr Hubbard told her stories and jokes during their daily journeys.

As for most children, the world of school opened many new vistas for Angela. Soon after she started, Mary had a telephone call from Mr Hollingshurst to say that when a teacher had offered to help Angela in her walk from the classroom to the hall, Angela had refused, politely but firmly, with the reply, "Thank you, Miss Tysoe, but I would rather try to make it under my own steam!"

This seemed to us to be typical of her attitude throughout her life.

Naturally, we were proud of all her achievements, physical and intellectual. She soon learned to read quite fluently, and it wasn't long before she asked if she could have a watch. I remember saying to her, "But sweetheart, you can't tell the time. As soon as you can I'll buy you a watch."

At this point she reminded me that I had often boasted of the time when I had taught Paul to tell the time in twenty minutes. (This was before the appearance of digital clocks and watches.)

"Well, if he could do it, why can't I?"

I decided that there was no answer to that so we set about there and then to master that skill. At the weekend, she got her watch.

As Christmas approached, she became very excited about

the school play. They were doing an adaptation of Long-fellow's poem, "The Song of Hiawatha". And she had a part! She didn't want to give us any details, as she wanted it all to be a surprise. But she did volunteer that it was a non-speaking part, so she didn't have the bother of learning lines. We duly attended the performance, and found that she had been cast in the role of the baby Hiawatha, and was on stage in a little crib for the whole play. Although hers was indeed a non-speaking part, she mouthed all of the words, for every part, throughout the whole of the play.

As well as the pleasure we experienced as we observed her intellectual development, we saw some improvement in the physical also. She had normal use of arms and right leg, and by the time she was six years old she had graduated from the frame to a pair of tripod sticks. These made her much more mobile, and it wasn't very long before she could manage on just one. This seemed to all of us progress indeed.

But one thing was giving us some cause for concern. Angela had started to complain of head pains. These were apparently mild at first, but it soon became obvious that they were getting more severe, and that something had to be done, beyond the administration of "home" remedies. The local doctor was call-ed, and he suggested that we take her to the nearest general hospital, Stafford Royal Infirmary. We attended there, but the staff there were just as baffled as the local doctor had been. Mary and I both had the same unspoken worry: was this going to be the start of another setback? Would it involve operations and painful treatment? How would Angela be able to cope with it all, especially the separation from Mary?

Our next journey to try to solve the problem of Angela's headaches took us to the General Hospital at Shrewsbury. Whilst she was being examined in another room, I was left alone. I looked out of the window, and saw beneath me a foot-ball ground, with terraces and stands around the playing area. I presumed that this was Shrewsbury Town's ground. As I contemplated my own sense of loneliness and worry, I saw a lone figure in a blue track suit begin to do laps of the field. He seemed so small against the comparative vastness of the

ground, and this reflected my sense of smallness and helpless-
ness when dealing with our current difficulties with our
daughter.

But our travels were not over yet, not by a long chalk. The
doctors there were not able to make a diagnosis, and told us to
go to the Oswestry Orthopaedic Hospital. I sighed with some
relief. At least, it wasn't very far to drive. There, after a long
examination, it was decided that the best place for her to obtain
treatment, was the Alder Hay Children's Hospital in Liverpool. There seemed to be much anxiety, and once the possibility of a helicopter being used was suggested. We were glad that
this idea was turned down because we would have been at
Liverpool, the car at Oswestry and as our home was near
Stafford, there would have been some difficulty.

So the doctors came to the conclusion that it would be all
right if Mary and I took her in the car. She was heavily sedated,
and slept peacefully on the back seat for the whole journey. I
was grateful that she had this interlude of oblivion before she
had to face the unknown at Liverpool.

At Alder Hay, there were more examinations, including X-
rays. We had thought that the tests at Oswestry were pro-
longed, but here the waiting seemed as if it would never end.
Before she was returned to us, we were confronted by three
doctors.

"I'm sorry you've both had a bit of a run around," said one,
"and we are also sorry to have kept you waiting for such a long
time, but there were so many different things we had to look
out for. Because your daughter has so many bodily malfunctions it has not been an easy task to find out exactly what the
cause of these headaches is. But now we are fairly confident
that we have discovered the cause."

He paused, as if he was waiting for all this to sink in. I was
aware of the relief in my mind that at last, after so many visits
to the various hospitals, we had finally arrived at a place where
Angela could get some help. I noticed some release of tension
in Mary's face too. The doctor continued.

"You perhaps know that in cases like this, there is always
present the possibility of a build up of cerebro-spinal fluid in

the spaces in the skull surrounding the brain. Well, that's what has now happened in Angela's head."

Again, another pause. I remembered that soon after she was born, someone had mentioned this possibility of hydro-cephalus, or "water on the brain". I had been very relieved that she hadn't suffered in this way, and there had certainly been no retardation in her intellectual development which would have accompanied such a condition. But this new turn of events re-vived the old fears. I had always believed that, even if little could be done to alleviate her physical condition, at least she would be able to get some kind of life fulfilment in the mental sphere.

I soon became aware of the doctor's voice again.

"We think that the pressure on the brain could well be relieved if we fit a special valve within the skull, which would drain off the excess fluid, taking away the pressure and the result would be the curing of the headaches. So, before I ask you to sign the consent form for the operation, are there any questions you would like to ask?"

My mind was in turmoil. The insertion of a valve into the head seemed a very drastic measure to me, but Mary spoke first.

"How successful is the operation likely to be? Is there no other treatment?"

"We cannot predict with any certainty the outcome of any surgery, particularly an operation such as this, which will take place so near the brain, but we can say that we have done many such procedures at this hospital, with a high percentage of suc-cess. And there is no other treatment which could help your little one."

I blurted out, "What would happen if nothing were done?"

"No-one can say with any certainty. But the chances are that the headaches would get worse, and her intellectual ability would diminish a great deal."

With such a prognosis we didn't seem to have much choice, and so the consent form was signed. Very reluctantly we signed Angela over to the care of the hospital authorities. Fortunately, we were able to explain to her that she was going to have an operation to get rid of her headaches, but we didn't go into any detail.

Immediately, Angela was prepared for the operation. The most distressing part of the process was that her head had to be shaved. She had very few attractive physical attributes, but she did have a lovely head of hair. We pacified her somewhat by telling her that when her hair grew again, it would be even thicker and stronger than it was then, and this seemed to ease her distress.

Soon she was whisked away and we were left to our own thoughts for what seemed ages, but I suppose was not more than two hours. One of the doctors returned to us with the news that the operation had been completed, and as far as they could tell, was successful. She was making a good recovery, and we would be able to see her in an hour's time.

When I got to see her I was shocked. Her head was swathed in bandages, and a small trickle of blood rolled down her left cheek. She was only just conscious, and the staff nurse assured us that everything was going to plan, so we tried to believe this – but it was not easy.

I had been granted a few days compassionate leave from the school, but I knew that this couldn't be extended indefinitely, and my absence would be putting a strain on my already much overworked colleagues. So Mary and I agreed that I should go back home that evening, and she would find some accommodation near the hospital. Thus she at least could visit as often as allowed. We discussed this with one of the nurses, who said, "But there's no need for you to go to that expense. I am sure you could stay in the Thalidomide Unit."

She went on to explain that when babies had been born with handicaps as a result of their mothers innocently taking the drug thalidomide, a special accommodation unit had been built so that parents could stay and be near their children while they were hospitalised. But now that this particular crisis had passed the unit could be used by any parent, and there were a number of vacant rooms. During the late evening I returned home, arranging to return to Liverpool the next evening.

I didn't sleep much that night. Paul had been taken to

Oldbury, to his grandparents, for a while, and so I was completely alone in the house, with nothing but my anxious thoughts for company.

But things often don't turn out as planned, and the next morning I had a frantic telephone call from Mary. No, there had gone nothing wrong with Angela, but from the room where she was, Mary could see the light on and much activity around Angela's bed, and this had distressed her very much. Mary had therefore decided that it would be better if she returned home and made the journey daily to Alder Hay. So, when school had finished for the day, I set off for Liverpool once more. Mary seemed much calmer now that she knew that she would be coming home to me each evening. Of course, we stayed with Angela until the last possible moment. She had now recovered from the effects of the anaesthetic and was able to chat away happily to us – and anyone else who would listen.

The next day, a Friday, established the pattern of Mary's activities for the next two weeks. Her first duty was to telephone the hospital at eight o'clock, and ask if Angela had had a good night. The nurse who answered would then tell her that her mum had rung. As Angela's bed was near the nurses' work station, she was aware each time the telephone rang.

As soon as the telephone call had been made, Mary would set off in the car for the sixty-six mile journey, and if she wasn't walking into the ward at ten o'clock precisely, Angela would tend to get a little upset. Then Mary would remain in the ward, helping to attend to Angela's needs until about eight o'clock in the evening, arriving home at about ten. At the weekends, of course, I was able to accompany her.

On the first Saturday, when Angela was really sitting up and taking notice, I asked her if there was anything she particularly wanted. After a few seconds' thought she said, "Yes, I think I would like a doll with long blond hair, if you can get me one."

I replied that we could surely respond to that simple request, and we left her, promising to return just as soon as the doll had been purchased.

We scoured all the local shops, but no doll with blond hair could be found. Finally, in desperation now because we had been out for much longer than we had anticipated, we saw one in a small, dark shop quite near to the hospital. Triumphantly we bore it to our daughter, who was delighted.

We all coped somehow with the problems of the next two weeks. But soon we were delighted to be told that Angela was now well enough to go home at the end of that week. Mary and I were so relieved: not only had Angela made such good progress that she could go home, but also we could now, at last, settle down to a normal family life. We could now give some attention to Paul, who we were anxious would not feel too neglected by being farmed out to his grandparents in Oldbury, forty miles away.

The Saturday when Angela was due to be discharged, was July 30th 1966, which, as all football fans will know, was the day that England were due to play West Germany in the final of the World Cup at Wembley. Although I am not, and never have been, a very keen watcher of soccer, I was rather eager to see the game on TV, in the hope of witnessing an English victory. So, on the journey from Liverpool, I put my foot down and arrived just in time for the kick off, and as we all know now, the English team was victorious. To me, it seemed a happy omen – victory for England, and victory for Angela.

CHAPTER 5

FRED GOES TO SCHOOL

Angela had been very happy at Blackfriars School, and she made good progress there. However, by now, after having taught for thirteen years, I thought it was time to be seeking promotion. After one unsuccessful effort, I landed the post of Deputy Head at Hunters' Hill School, at the small village of Blackwell, near Bromsgrove, Worcestershire. This was a City of Birmingham Residential School for "delicate" boys aged eight to sixteen. There were a hundred and four boys in residence on average and most of them were far from being delicate. However, many did display problems of behaviour, and working there tended to use up most of one's energies. But it was a very rewarding job.

Angela was now presenting problems at school. We had enrolled her at a day special school, about ten miles from our new home. She was very unhappy there, and for some months neither Mary nor I was able to fathom out why this was so. But Angela did complain from time to time of unsympathetic treatment, particularly from one of the teaching staff. For some time I took little notice of these complaints, having observed for many years how children can manipulate their parents with stories of unkind treatment at school. So on many occasions Angela would complain of feeling ill first thing in the morning. We were often in the dilemma of not knowing whether these were cases of genuine sickness. It is difficult enough when dealing with any child who exhibits symptoms of mild school phobia, but with a child who had so many congenital handicaps as our daughter, decisions as to whether to send her to school or not were particularly hard. On the whole, I think we erred on the side of hardness, and looking back, I feel sure that we sometimes insisted on her going to school when she was unwell.

In due course, however, the real cause of her distress became apparent. One day, after much questioning, she told us the truth.

At first, she had been quite happy at the new school. She had made friends quickly, and found the work quite within her capabilities. But an incident occurred which changed all that. Although she was by now more or less self sufficient as far as handling her incontinence problems were concerned, there was still the possibility of the occasional "accident". And one of these happened one day in class. There appeared on the floor a small puddle near Angela's feet. Now, one would have thought that, being in a school for physically handicapped pupils, with its small classes, the teacher would have been aware of the special problems of all of the children in her class. But, apparently, this was not so. Instead of showing some understanding of the situation, she scolded Angela quite severely in front of the rest of the children. Thus, Angela had been afraid to go to school, because she never quite knew if the situation would occur again.

It was left to Mary to go to the school and sort out the problem. Although there was a grudging apology, I was having second thoughts about the suitability of the school for our daughter. The general level of attainments of the children was, I felt, very low, and it seemed that Angela was not being stretched to work at her full capacity. So, eventually, we decided to remove her. The next problem was, to which school should we send her? One rather obvious solution was proposed by the head of the school at which I taught – that Angela should attend this school. There were many advantages. There would be no transport costs as we lived on site. There would be no question of understanding her problems, and either Mary or I would always be near to give help and support as necessary. The main disadvantage was that it was an all boys school, and whilst Angela got on well with the boys, and in fact spent most of her out-of-school hours in their company, it was rather a question of how the local education authority would view the matter.

The head, however, was quite adamant. She was now at the end of her long and distinguished career, and she was quite prepared to buck authority. Linda Buckley had been at the school for thirty-three years, the last twenty odd as head. This was no mean achievement at a school which had more than its quota of boys with behaviour problems. She ran the school with a firm but kindly discipline. All in all she was a formidable person, and I think took upon herself the responsibility of admitting Angela to the school, without any reference to higher authority.

So Angela settled into the life of Hunters' Hill school. Of course, she already knew the pupils and staff. And how she loved going to classes there!

Only one thing bothered the boys. How, they argued with me, can we have a name like Angela, on the roll of a boys' school? The solution was obvious to them. She would have to change her name. So thereafter she was known as "Fred".

Although I never had her in one of my classes (she was in the lower school, whilst I taught the oldest boys), I soon received reports from the teachers concerned, about the high standard of work she was showing. It made me consider very seriously where she should be educated from the age of eleven. Quite clearly, the present arrangement could only be regarded as temporary, and a more permanent one must soon be found.

After three months, and much negotiation with her previous day school, we agreed that she should return on a part time basis. This proved to be satisfactory, although Angela would have preferred to stay at Hunters', as the school was known locally. In a matter of a few weeks, she was ready to attend full time, and seemed quite able to cope with it.

In the meantime, Paul had sat the old eleven plus examination, and was attending the grammar school at Bromsgrove. He loved living at Hunters', as he always had plenty to do in the evenings and at weekends. It was good to see that he had no resentment at the amount of attention we had to give to his sister, and in later years he confirmed this himself. By this time, he was strong enough to help with lifting and pushing her wheelchair, which she had to use for a walk of more than about a hundred yards.

At this time too, when Angela was eight years old, she began to take more of an interest in social activities. One of her ambitions was to join the Brownies, and we found a local group that welcomed her as a member. Because she was so short, we had to have her uniform made to measure. She was so proud to have a uniform to wear!

In 1967 we had bought a touring caravan, a Sprite Musketeer. In this and the following year we had several lovely holidays. During our first year with a "tourer" we decided to go to Scotland for five weeks, and to break this up with a week at Butlin's, Ayr, during the middle part of the holiday. Angela and Paul had a marvellous week there. The Redcoats made sure that she was not left out of anything. They even encouraged her to take part in a junior talent competition, having sought our permission first. She was very nervous, but sang her song well and was awarded second prize – a free holiday for herself next year. Naturally, we couldn't disappoint her, so in 1968 the Powell family again sallied forth to Ayr. In the meantime, we had exchanged the caravan for a slightly larger one.

The next year, 1969, we decided to go a little further afield. We studied books and brochures, and settled on a tour of the coast of Ireland. (In late July of that year there was little trouble.) It was indeed a very wise decision, and apart from a slight worsening of the political situation towards the end of the holiday, there was not much to complain about. However, for Angela, and therefore for us, the highlight of the tour was undoubtedly the week we spent in the county of Donegal.

It was the third week of our holiday when we arrived at Donegal, and we were delighted to discover that it was festival week. There were many events which were of interest, but the one which fascinated Angela was the beauty contest. We attended every night, and on the last night, when the grand final took place, we were all delighted when the winner made a short speech and presented Angela with a musical Teddy bear! We were pleased with this unexpected, warm-hearted gesture. Twenty-two years later, the Teddy still is in pristine condition.

The time had arrived for Miss Buckley to retire (she was approaching her sixty-fifth birthday). The post was advertised, and I applied. Naturally, as the Deputy Head, I stood a good chance, and I was very keen to get the job. However, it was not to be, and I, in perhaps an uncharacteristic fit of pique, applied for the post of headmaster at Warlies, a residential school for physically handicapped children of secondary age, in Essex. The school was run by Barnardo's. After several interviews and visits, both to the school, and to the Barnardo headquarters at Barkingside, Ilford, I learned that my application had been successful. So towards the end of December 1970, we said goodbye to all our friends at Hunters' and took up residence at Warlies.

Angela's schooling was now no problem. She attended "my" school. I have known many teachers who would not have any of their children attend the school at which they taught at any price. Personally, I could never understand this attitude. I would have been thrilled to have had either of my children in the same school as myself, but the opportunity never occurred with Paul. There were some snags though.

Although my duties as the head were very time consuming, and left me with little time for teaching, I did my best to spend some time in each of the four classrooms every week. Also, during times of staff illness, I had no alternative but to act as a supply teacher. If I happened to take Angela's class, she would often, after school, offer her criticisms of my lessons, or the way I happened to handle a particular situation! She also indicated that, in order that I should not be thought to be favouring my daughter, I was rather stricter with her than I was with the other children. Still, I think I learned much about the attitudes of the pupils to their school and staff. Angela was very contented there, and of course there was always plenty of company during out-of-school hours.

But, happy as she was, I became convinced that Warlies was not the place for her. I had always envisaged that, in spite of her disabilities, she would grow up to live her adult life as a contributing, independent member of society. And, I couldn't see that happening if she received the rest of her education in the protected environment of a residential special school. So I started to give this problem some serious thought. I think this period was a kind of watershed in Angela's life. What was to happen over the next few years would set the tone of the whole of the rest of her life.

From the general level of her intellectual ability, I came to the conclusion that she ought to attend a school where the attainments of the children were greater than those of the pupils at Warlies. I knew of a boarding school in Hampshire, the Lord Mayor Treloar School, which offered a grammar school education for pupils with physical handicaps. Now I knew that Angela would suffer terrible emotional problems if sent away to school, and even if there were benefits in the long term, Mary and I were not prepared to put Angela and ourselves through the turmoil of separation. We considered all the angles. Perhaps I might be able to get a job as a teacher at the school. Maybe if that were not possible I could get a job at a school nearby and Angela could attend the Lord Mayor Treloar as a day pupil.

These ideas, and many others, circulated in our minds for a couple of months or so. And, as so often happens, the solution came quite out of the blue. At Warlies, we had a female physiotherapist. One day, in casual conversation with Mary, she said that her own secondary education had been received at a Roman Catholic Grammar School at Woodford, which was only a few miles from Warlies. The school's head was a nun, and a number of the teachers were also. The physio was sure that Angela would receive sympathetic treatment there. This seemed to be the answer to our prayers – if all the arrangements could be made. First of all we made an appointment to see the head, Sister Mary Joseph. After some days, she rang up to say that, after consultation with the staff, and I assumed governors too, she had decided to offer Angela a place, subject to a satisfactory performance in the eleven plus test. So this was to be the next hurdle.

The question now was, would she do well enough in the test to gain a grammar school place? She would be in competition with children who had none of her handicaps. Also, many of these pupils would have received special pre-examination coaching, which although specifically against the local education authority's rules, went on, I knew, in many schools.

So, arrangements were made with the Essex Education Committee for Angela to take the eleven plus. (As she was a pupil in a special school, this was not compulsory, as it was for all pupils attending primary schools.) As it was customary for children to sit the test in their own schools, Angela would sit the single-paper examination at Warlies. I had decided against any special coaching as I wanted to play the whole thing strictly by the rules. If she did get a grammar school place, I wanted it to be entirely on her own merit.

Eventually, the dreaded paper arrived. I had tried to play down the importance of the test to Angela, but I was very worked up about it. The test arrived by post, a few days before it was to be administered. Inside the outer envelope was an inner with the words "Not to be opened before . . ." printed on it. I can tell you that the temptation to open it and practise the questions with Angela was almost overwhelming. But, somehow, I managed to resist it. It occurred to me that if I supervised the test alone with Angela, I laid myself open to the charge of cheating, so I arranged for one of the teaching staff, Hugh Parrot, to be in the room with Angela and myself, whilst the test was taken.

Afterwards, I faced another strong temptation – to go through the test and alter wrong answers. With difficulty I resisted this also. The test was sent off, unamended by me, and we settled down to a period of anxious waiting – well, Mary and I were anxious anyway.

The letter came, weeks later. I knew without having to open it what it would contain. The only contact I had had with the Education Office at Chelmsford had been with regard to our daughter's secondary school placement. But would the news be good? I was too anxious to open it, so I called in Mary to do it for me. She found it difficult to understand what was written as it was couched in education jargon, so she handed the letter to me. The form letter stated that Angela had scored 226. The "pass" for a boy was 224, and for a girl 228. So, in spite of all our hopes, our little girl would not be able to take her place in the mainstream of the educational system. I put the letter down on the office desk. I looked out of the window at the clump of trees to avoid looking at Mary's eyes. When I did manage to meet her gaze, I could tell she was doing her best not to cry.

We thought it was best to wait until the end of the school day before telling Angela. Mary went up to our flat and I was left alone with my brooding thoughts. Only two marks short of a place in a normal girls' grammar school! If only I had cheated just a little. Just one more question correct would have clinched it. I picked up the letter again. Maybe I had misread the letter. It's easy to do that when you're as excited and anxious as I had been. But, as I re-read the note, I saw that I had made no mistake. However, I had not read to the end. There was a sort of postscript. Because Angela had scored very nearly a pass mark, she qualified for a re-sit.

Mary and I couldn't make up our minds whether this news was a new opportunity, or another invitation to anxiety. But when we told Angela, she seemed quite unperturbed. So, three weeks later, she was once more ensconced with Hugh and me in a vacant classroom, struggling with the questions on the examination paper.

Once again, a worrying wait, but this time a satisfactory result. Angela had done well enough to gain a place in an "ordinary" grammar school. Her own personal fight for normality had really begun.

Chapter 6

GAMES

Arrangements were quickly made for a taxi to take Angela to her new school, the Holy Family Convent School, Woodford. The journey took about twenty-five minutes. As at Standon, we were extremely fortunate with the driver. He was a cheerful, outgoing chap, Dave Cakebread. We were all very amused at his, to us, unusual surname, and over the next few years he became very important to us. This was the first time that Angela had ever attended an "ordinary" school, and Dave's good humour certainly helped Angela to adjust to her new and, for her, sometimes trying circumstances. She felt the transition difficult in many ways. The day was long. The parting from Mary each day was traumatic. She had to cope with a large school, with watching the girls play energetic games which she couldn't join in, and with having to work at full stretch to keep up with the others – something she had never had to bother about before. All these factors, and many more, combined to make life trying for her. I was aware of most of the problems, but I didn't have to face up to them each day, as Angela did.

But the staff of the school did everything they could to ease the burden on her. Towards the end of the summer term the head had invited me to speak to the girls about the new pupil who was to start in September. I found it a bit intimidating myself to be confronted with several hundred girls, after so long in schools of about a hundred or less, so I could imagine how tricky it was going to be for Angela. Still, I overcame my nervousness, and spoke for about twenty minutes. The main points I emphasised were the temptations to help her too much, and the fact of her incontinence. A special toilet was to be made available which would have a cupboard to store the pads, and would be used solely by Angela. The other special provision concerned domestic science. Because she was so short, this subject had been impossible for her even at Warlies, and she seemed so keen to do it. So the head had a special low unit made which contained a sink, cooker and work surface. She could now study domestic science to "O" level standard.

In order to make her feel a little less left out of things, the staff encouraged her to take an interest in the rules of tennis, and, although she couldn't play, she became much in demand as an umpire. The staff did these and many other things to make her feel at home.

One subject that did cause her concern was French. I couldn't quite understand this, as she was happy with her other language, Spanish. The only pointer was perhaps a slight clash of personality with the teacher. The matter was brought home to me rather dramatically one day when Dave rang up to ask if we could do the transport ourselves, as he was not well. I drove her, and we were about a mile from the school when she suddenly started to cry. I stopped the car and asked what the matter was. She didn't speak, but pointed to a flag flying from the head office of a building firm. The flag bore the name of the firm "French". She quickly recovered her composure, and we both had a good laugh about the incident. But the thought that she might have even one moment of unhappiness plagued me then and throughout her life, even though I realised that there were many situations in which I was powerless to help.

By now, Angela was able to take an interest in most adult concerns. The plight of starving people in Africa was one that made her very sad, for instance. Her intelligent interest in a great number of things made her a good companion for Mary and me. Paul at this time was very much involved with his girl friend, Gill, and didn't spend too much time in the bosom of his family. They had met at a Salvation Army meeting. Mary had become involved with the Army, and Paul and Angela used to go along with her. Mary and I loved the company of our daughter, who at the age of twelve had become an excellent conversationalist. So, when the question of holidays came up, there was never any doubt that she should go with us. In any case, we could never have enjoyed a vacation apart from her.

The most ambitious trip we went on was a visit to the United States. Mary has a married sister living near Philadelphia, and at her invitation we flew in a VC10 from Heathrow towards the end of July 1973. Angela was now thirteen and I suggested that she might like to keep a diary of the trip in a school exercise book. During the flight, to pass the time away, she began to write her notes. One of the stewards saw what she was doing, and asked if she would like to visit the flight deck, to see how the aircraft was controlled. Because she found walking about in the narrow aisle a little difficult, I went with her. She and I spent a fascinating quarter of an hour talking to the flight crew, and marvelling at their skill. During the flight, Philadelphia Airport was radioed to make sure that a wheelchair would be available for Angela. And it was. Also an attendant was with it to push. On the many occasions when we travelled by air we invariably found that the airport staff were extremely helpful. The trip to America took in Niagara Falls, and was very successful for us. Paul came with us, somewhat reluctantly because he and Gill were now very serious about their relationship and were already talking about marriage.

Encouraged by the school, Angela became keen on watching tennis. Whenever a match was on television, she would be glued to the square screen. She became familiar with the star players, styles of play and many of the more intricate features of play. We managed to get tickets for three Wimbledon men's finals for "Miss A. Powell and escort". As the most convenient way to get to Wimbledon was by tube, Mary felt that it was better for me to go with Angela. Although I was not too keen on tennis, I thoroughly enjoyed the electric atmosphere, and greatly admired the skill and fitness of players such as Borg, Connors and McEnroe.

Bjorn Borg had now become a sporting hero to Angela. She collected photographs, books and stories as some girls might have about film or pop stars. Angela was interested in these too, but it was Borg who received her greatest adulation.

Every year, in the autumn, there was, and still may be, an

indoor tournament at Wembley, the Benson and Hedges. Our practice had been for a few years to take Angela and a school friend to Wembley, drop them off at about one o'clock, and go off to see some friends. We would return for the girls at ten o'clock and bring them home. The tournament would be almost over by then, and the stewards would let Mary and me in to see the final stages of the last match. On one occasion, when we met the girls, we found Angela in a state of profound excitement.

"Dad, you'll never guess what I've done! I've spent fifteen minutes in Bjorn's dressing room, and look, he's given me this ball, and he's signed it!"

I was dumbfounded. How could this tiny girl, who could barely walk, have managed to penetrate the high security which surrounds all high profile sportsmen?

"But how did you manage that?"

"I simply asked one of the stewardesses if she could possibly get me his autograph. She went away with my book, and when she came back she said he would like to see me. So she took me to him and that's what happened. But you should see the dressing rooms. They're ever so dingy!"

This was just one occasion when I was surprised at Angela's initiative and complete self confidence.

Paul and Gill had now been seeing each other for several years, in spite of the fact that they were both only eighteen. I can't recall Paul having any other girl friend, at least he never told me of any others. Our family had become very friendly with Gill's and when the subject of the marriage came up we all agreed that although they were quite young, they were quite mature in their outlook, and we would support them in any way we could.

Warlies was somewhat isolated from any form of public transport, and I used to allow a suitable member of the residential child care staff to use the mini-bus for off-duty outings to local places of entertainment. On one particular occasion, one child care worker came up to me and said, "Mr Powell, you know you've said we can have the minibus to go to the pictures tomorrow night, well, we were wondering if perhaps Paul would like to come with us."

"I don't know, but I'll ask him and let you know. By the way, what film are you going to see?"

"I don't know yet. I don't even know what's on. But there's bound to be something reasonable on somewhere."

Paul decided that he would go with the group. Apart from his almost daily outings with Gill, he hardly ever went out with people of his own age, and I thought this outing might do him some good.

He returned home quite late, and in a terrible emotional state. The film was *The Exorcist*. I had had no idea that such a film had been made, so out of touch was I about what went on in the outside world. Even if I had known, I don't think I would have prevented Paul from going. He was such a level headed boy, who had benefitted much from the influence of the Salvation Army teaching, particularly in their attitudes to smoking, drink and drugs. He was about as stable as you could expect any eighteen-year-old to be. But, after seeing the film, he was in such a state of terror that he was afraid to sleep on his own. Angela offered a spare bed in her room, and it was there that he slept until he was married. Angela also helped his emotional health considerably whilst he was still living with us.

Paul and Gill had now definitely decided to get married, and as the summer of '74 progressed, arrangements for the wedding went on apace. The ceremony was to take place at the lovely old church in Waltham Abbey, and the reception in the school hall at Warlies. Mary took great delight in assuming responsibility for most of the arrangements.

Angela was very excited at the prospect of the forthcoming event. She was to be one of three bridesmaids, the other two being Gill's twin sisters, who were the same age as Angela. However, she was concerned with one thing – the possibility of wearing shoes. She had had to wear boots ever since she had started to walk, because they were needed to support the metal calliper required to provide strength to the weakened leg. Mary and I couldn't quite see how the boots could be dispensed with, but, on a routine visit to the Children's Hospital, Hackney, the examining doctor gave us some hope that it might be possible.

But, as the foot tended to turn out, sideways, an operation would be needed first. This would involve putting a pin into the knee, and the fitting of a plastic, not metal calliper. Much as we didn't want Angela to undergo further surgery, we discussed the matter with her, and it was her decision to have it done. In due course the operation proceeded without any undue trauma, and the calliper fitted. This plastic one was much lighter than the one made of metal, and meant that Angela could now do something she had longed to do for a long time – go into an ordinary shoe shop, and choose a pair for herself. The joy she took in doing this was very great indeed. The bridesmaids had chosen to wear white shoes, so Angela had to choose two pairs, one for the wedding, and another pair for everyday wear. For the latter, she chose brown. The calliper fitted around her foot, inside the shoe, so no alteration to the footwear was necessary, other than a very small build up.

It certainly was a great day for all of us when, on October 12th 1974, a day before Paul's nineteenth birthday, the wedding took place. The officiating minister was a curate, Ian Pusey, who was to be present at a few more significant events in the Powell family's life.

After the wedding the happy couple went to live in Birmingham, with Mary's mother, who was a widow. During the next year or so, Angela was in demand as a bridesmaid in three weddings. She was now beginning to think of the prospect of her own marriage, but because of her physical problems, I thought this possibility to be remote. So, to prevent, as I thought, future disappointment, I discouraged any such talk. But she still had her own private thoughts and dreams.

It became clear that the strain of residential work was beginning to tell on the family. Mary was working as a domestic bursar, and we rarely saw one another except at bedtimes. But, as so often happens in life, we were too involved with work to see that the true values of family life were being slowly eroded. It took Angela to help us to see that we were missing out on a great deal by the kind of work we were doing.

We were having tea together, a rare occurrence, when she said, "I'd like us to go to the Royal Tournament."

"Yes, we are going. I've arranged to take all the children," I put in quickly.

"But I want us to go."

It took me a few minutes to understand what she meant. She wanted us to go out as a normal family, without the company of the forty other children of our "extended" family. This brought home to me the fact that she didn't always want to share her parents with the other children. It also made me think very carefully and long about our future in residential work. I couldn't realise at the time the amount of damage it was doing to our marriage and family life, but Angela's remark about the Royal Tournament was bringing me gradual realisation that useful as the work was, residential work was taking its toll.

Actually, events beyond our control made the decision easier. For some time, Barnardo's had plans for a new purpose-built school to be established in the Barnardo "village" at Barkingside, a part of Ilford in Essex. None of us fancied the move from an idyllic spot in the middle of Epping Forest to the urban sprawl which is Barkingside. So, one evening, the three of us sat down to consider our future. The facts were: I was forty-five years old, hopefully still young enough to consider a change; the proposed move to Barkingside from our point of view was not beneficial; we had had enough of residential work anyway, and I wanted a change. What I really wanted was a return to primary school work.

So, it was decided. I would seek a headship in the primary sector. Of course, there was the problem of housing. I am afraid we had been rather wasteful of money during the past fifteen years, with very little saved. I was therefore looking for a job with accommodation. Apart from boarding schools, the only ones I had ever heard of that had school houses were a few small, rural schools in remote areas. Perusing the now defunct *Teachers' World*, I applied for the post of Head Teacher at the small school at Baconsthorpe, a hamlet about twenty five miles north of Norwich. I was successful, and as a house went with the job, it was a good move to make.

CHAPTER 7

GETTING ABOUT

Baconsthorpe proved to be a delightful village to live in. There was space, tranquillity and a job for me in which the only problems were purely educational ones. However, we had to deal with the difficulty of continuing Angela's education. Now that she had made such a good start to her secondary schooling, we wanted to make sure that this foundation was not wasted.

There were two grammar schools in the area. Both were a considerable distance from our new home, and to be honest, neither seemed very keen to admit a pupil with as many physical difficulties as Angela would present. Both heads seemed overly concerned with the possibility of accidents, although in both cases I offered to take out personal insurance which would have absolved the schools of all accident responsibility. Although we could have insisted that she was admitted to either of these schools, clearly we would not have wanted her to have attended a place where she would not be enthusiastically welcomed.

Then, as we were contemplating the problem, inspiration struck. Mary remembered that when we were at Warlies, one of the teachers, Roy Kerridge, used to tell us about his experiences at Gresham's, the public school in Holt. In fact, Roy's father had been a teacher there, and had been responsible for the construction of the open air theatre. This seemed to offer a possible solution. In Roy's day, the school catered only for boys, but when we made inquiries, we discovered that a small number of girls were now attending. As Gresham's is situated only just over three miles from Baconsthorpe, we thought it was worth going into the possibility of Angela attending there. I had no idea at all as to whether the head and staff would be sympathetic to her application to join the school.

The head at that time was Logie Bruce-Lockhart. We made an appointment to see him with Angela, and found him to be sympathetic to our cause. Indeed, he seemed very keen to have Angela in his school. I felt it was rather important for him to realise that she would not present too many problems, pointing out that she had never had an accident at school, and she had been at school for eleven years. Just after I had made this statement, I was carrying Angela up a staircase, and fell with her in my arms. Fortunately, neither of us were hurt, and the accident didn't prejudice Angela's chances. Bruce-Lockhart was a warm, caring headmaster, and the three of us warmed to him almost immediately. Later, I discovered that he had played rugby for Scotland, and that knowledge increased my respect for him even more.

When the interview and tour of the school had ended, he said he would gladly admit Angela to the school as a day pupil, subject to the confirmation of the school governors. He did not anticipate any problem with them, and in due course his decision was ratified by the governors and Angela prepared herself for the difficult transition to a new school.

At the time, I don't think I fully realised how difficult ordinary life was for Angela. At Gresham's, they certainly pulled out all the stops to make her school life as pleasant as possible. The boys in her form worked on a rota system to push her in her wheelchair to the various departments of the building, and, when Mary and I visited, they seemed to be glad that they were of service to her in this way. One of these was a lad named Nick Youngs – later to achieve great things on the rugby field, culminating in his being capped for England. Angela and I were very thrilled to see him playing on the television, and I am sure that Mr Bruce-Lockhart shared in this admiration too. But, in spite of all the goodwill shown to her, she had to miss out on many of the activities, mainly on the sports field. She never complained about this, but I wonder how much she resented her physical limitations without saying anything to anyone.

There was one activity which I thought she would never be

able to take part in, woodwork. But the teacher of this subject, Mr Burroughs, known to all very affectionately as "Jumbo", gave her a great deal of encouragement, and the highlight of her association with planes and chisels was when she indicated that her woodwork "job" was ready to bring home. When I collected it I was very surprised to find that she had made a quite lovely coffee table. What was even more surprising was that Mr Burroughs informed me that she had made it with the very minimum of help! The table has seen a lot of use, and is still in daily service today.

There was one disappointing deficiency in the curriculum as far as Angela was concerned. There was no Spanish course. At her previous school, she had done three years of this language, and she had acquired a fair degree of proficiency in it. Therefore it had become one of her favourite subjects. She had had some practice too. During our fairly frequent holidays in Spain, she was our interpreter. Quite often, but especially the time when we toured the southern part of the country in our caravan, we surprised an unsuspecting native by winding the car window down to ask for directions. They were most surprised to find themselves being addressed in reasonable Spanish by this little scrap of a girl. And of course she enjoyed all this knowledge a great deal. I think part of the enjoyment was being able to do something much better than Dad could do it.

The staff and pupils at Gresham's certainly did their best to ensure that Angela's stay there was both happy and profitable. At the end of her time there, she had gained six "O" levels with good grades and this result brought a lot of satisfaction to all the family. But by this time in her life she was beginning to realise that there was more to life than school. The talk amongst her study mates at school was of boy friends, future marriage and children, and none of this seemed within the reach of a teenaged girl who was so disabled.

Another handicap which we did not pay much attention to at this point in her life was her short stature. She had attained a height of less than four feet, and this was to be a crucial stumbling block to her efforts to live a full life later on.

I was getting more than a little concerned about Angela's social life. She was spending almost all her leisure time in our company, and was always taken with us on our social outings. Whilst she seemed quite happy to be with us, and she took a full part in any conversation, it seemed to me that a girl in her late teens ought to be more often in the company of people of her own age. Although Mary and I were always on hand to provide transport to wherever she wanted to go, these occasions were too few and far between.

I had heard of a club whose aim is to bring together those who have physical disabilities and those who are able bodied. One evening, when we were talking around the fire, I asked, "Angela, wouldn't you like to go to one of these clubs where you would meet people?"

From her expression I could tell that she didn't think much of the idea. But over the next few days I kept on sowing the seeds of this notion, and eventually she agreed to allow Mary to take her.

The evening for the meeting came, and with some trepidation, I watched them leave. Mary had been in favour of the suggestion, and I suspected that Angela agreed to go merely to please her mother. The meeting was held about an hour's drive from home, and so it was quite late when I heard our car draw up outside the house.

The expression on their faces told me everything I wanted to know about their evening. Angela said, "Dad, don't ever suggest that I should go there or anywhere like that ever again!"

It seemed that she had been treated by some of the able bodied members as someone who was a second class citizen in every way. From this point on, Mary and I respected Angela's wishes, and she never again ever had anything to do with organisations for handicapped people. It seemed to me also that if she was going to lead anything approaching a life with the normal expectation, she would have to make it on her own, with her own efforts.

We now had to consider the next stage in her education. She had no desire at all to continue into the sixth form and take some "A" levels, and we spent several weeks discussing, at any odd moment, what Angela might like to do next. By now, Mary and I had stopped telling our daughter what we thought would be best for her. Instead, we encouraged her to think for herself and make her own arrangements for her future, relying on our help only when she really needed it, and when she requested it. She had for a long time been interested in the medical profession and would have loved to have become a nurse. Unfortunately, her disabilities precluded this choice. However, we all thought she might make it as a medical secretary, and it so happened that there was a suitable course at the college of technology in Norwich, twenty-five miles from our home at Baconsthorpe.

So in due course enquiries were made, application forms filled in and interviews attended. We were all quite overwhelmed when, a few weeks after Angela attended the interviews, she received a letter from the Norwich City College stating that she had been accepted for a place on the medical secretaries course. This was a two-year course leading to the diploma. Again, the local education authority gave us very good support in supplying a taxi each day for the journey to Norwich.

The two years passed without any incident of note, which showed Mary and me that our daughter could make it in the world, without the need for special provision. Of course, she did have a great deal of help from her fellow students and tutors. Indeed, we had the privilege of meeting several of her colleagues, and they were all very friendly. One rather special friend, Alison Jones, became very dear to us and Angela. In fact she still keeps in touch with us periodically. I think Angela fitted in very well at the college, and, at the end of the course, passed the final examination.

During her last few months at the college we had another problem to solve. If she were to be independent of us, she would have to get a job. And this would require her to be independent of us for transport. We racked our brains to see how we could possibly afford a car for her. We ourselves had only a very old car, and there was no way that we could see our way clear to buy one for Angela. It seemed that her way to an independent life was blocked, and we seemed to be up against a brick wall. The only thing to be done was to apply for one of those funny-looking three-wheeled vehicles which the government was then supplying to handicapped people – the Invacar.

In order to qualify for one of these, an application had to be made, which was followed by a visit from a doctor. He spent some time with Mary and Angela, administering various tests of mobility, and asking many questions. We didn't get the decision there and then, but were told that we would be informed in due course, by post.

We were in no anxiety over this, as we had seen many people, not nearly as handicapped as Angela was, driving Invacars. We waited for the application to be considered, believing that it was merely a formality that had to be endured. It certainly would mean a lot to Angela to be able to get about under her own steam. She would be able to come and go as she pleased, not always to be dependent on her parents for her outings.

We were all deeply shocked when the result of the application arrived. It had been turned down on the grounds that Angela's mobility was too great to warrant the granting of one of the government's cars for disabled people. We were in a state of shock for several days. Angela could walk only a few yards, and then only indoors where the floor was perfectly level and there were no adverse weather conditions. If the slightest wind blew on her, or if the ground were even slightly wet, then she was liable to fall down. Also, because of her shortness, she was unable to use public transport even if there were any available. In Baconsthorpe, there were only two buses a week.

However, the letter which gave us the bad news did hold out one ray of hope. We could appeal to a special tribunal, and we could be represented by a lawyer if we so desired. We decided to appeal, and secured the services of a member of the staff of a well known local firm of solicitors. The appeal before the tribunal was a farce. Angela, Mary and I found it most humiliating. Angela was asked to walk around the rather large table, which of course she could do. The lawyer was hopeless. His powers of argument seemed to be almost nil. He had no idea of the problems of the disabled, and quite honestly, I could have done a lot better myself. We had engaged him only because we thought the panel would be more impressed with his persuasion than with the arguments we could produce. So it was no surprise to us when we heard that the appeal had been turned down. I suspect that the reason for this was not to do with Angela's disabilities, but that the panel thought that I ought to be able to supply a vehicle myself, and thus save the government the cost. It all made me feel very guilty, but I simply did not have the funds to do anything about it. I imagine that people found this hard to believe, but this was the absolute truth.

It seemed that bureaucracy had once again interfered with our plans for our daughter to begin to have a more or less independent life and career. We felt more frustrated than ever. Angela had every prospect of leaving the City College in a few months with a recognised qualification, but she would not be able to take up an appointment because of lack of transport. Of course, either Mary or I might have been able to take Angela to and from work, but this would have been dependent on where she obtained employment, and the hours she would be working. We felt that we were unable to do any more to make Angela less dependent on us. But, once again, a higher authority overruled in the matter.

By some means or other (we never did discover how), one of the local district councillors, Mrs Judith Walpole, had found out about our predicament. She came to see us and, after a long discussion, agreed to start a fund to raise sufficient money to buy Angela a car. Judith suggested that she opened her home, Mannington Hall, to the public on a Sunday afternoon, and charge for admission. This was a brilliant idea, and if successful it would mean Angela would have an ordinary car, and not an Invacar, which would not have been all that satisfactory on two counts. First, they were not all that reliable; second, no passengers could be carried, which meant that wherever she went, she would always have to be alone.

The afternoon was a huge success. The sum of five hundred pounds was raised, which in 1977 was worth a lot more than it is now. This was a marvellous start for the fund and it also generated much publicity. This stimulated a great deal of interest, and there were many offers of help from church groups, public houses and schools. One of the more unusual offers came from the Magpie, a public house in Norwich. The customers there were most helpful, and in particular two pensioners, known as Snowy and Tom. These two, almost seventy years old, proposed to ride their bicycles right around the coastline of mainland Britain, a total of over four thousand miles. They were to collect for the car on the way. I thought that this was far too hazardous an undertaking for men of their years, but they would not be dissuaded, and they completed their ride, raising a considerable amount in the process. Mary and I were so impressed with their effort that we nominated them for the "Hearts of Gold" competition run by the *Sunday People*. They weren't the winners, but they were runners up, and with Mary and Angela were invited to a lunch at one of the top London hotels. The efforts of Snowy and Tom received much publicity, which in turn sparked off other people to think of different schemes to make the car a possibility. After what seemed a very short time there was sufficient in the fund to make the purchase.

The type of car which would suit Angela needed a lot of thinking about. It would have to be small. It would need a raised floor, as her legs would not have been able to reach the pedals; in fact these would need to be extended upwards through the false floor. The driver's seat would have to be raised, to enable her to see through the windscreen. And it would have to have a boot large enough to take her folding wheelchair. Also, it would have to have automatic transmission, as her left leg was almost completely paralysed, and was not strong enough to have operated a clutch. There was one car on the market that fitted all these conditions, a Mini Clubman. A local dealer offered to supply, and in due course Mary and I collected the Mini from their Great Yarmouth branch. It must have been frustrating for Angela not being able to drive, but she didn't complain (well, not much!).

A local firm specialising in vehicle adaptations did the conversion, and when the work was complete we were delighted that Angela could manage all the controls perfectly. Luckily, the amount of money collected was sufficient to pay for all the alterations. We contacted a driving instructor, Roland Nurse, and to our astonishment he offered to teach her for half the usual fee.

She appeared to learn quite quickly. When she had had a few lessons, and could control the car reasonably well, Mary and I would take her out for practice. One manoeuvre she found particularly tricky was reversing. This was because the shape of her back prevented her from turning round in a sitting position. This meant that all her reversing was done using the mirror, and if you've ever tried this you'll know just how difficult it is. So, whenever I took her out, I made sure she had plenty of practice in this skill.

After a fair number of lessons, Roland told us that he thought she was now ready to take the test. This was the same rigorous test that every would-be driver has to take. Already she had been given much practice by Roland in Norwich, and she didn't seem to face the prospect of the test with too much trepidation. As she was often to point out to me, I myself had taken three tries to pass, so she wouldn't be too disappointed if she didn't pass first time. The day of the test came, and none of the family was surprised by the fact that when Angela came home the "L" plates were still in position on her car. But, when we examined the 'Failed' certificate, we could see that she had failed only on a few minor points. Angela was in a way quite pleased with her performance, and not disheartened in the slightest. In fact, I suppose it would be true to say that the entire family were very pleased with Angela's effort, and we all encouraged her to be stimulated to greater endeavours.

The lessons with Roley Nurse continued, perhaps with more visits to the test routes in Norwich than had been previously made. Immediately after the first test she had applied for another, and it was only a few weeks later that she was undergoing the ordeal again. At least, it seemed like an ordeal to me. I remembered my own tests, more than twenty years before, and how nervous I had been. I believed I had some excuse for my second failure, as on that day Angela had been undergoing surgery on her spine, and with the waiting lists for driving tests being so long in the West Midlands, I thought I had better go through with it. I did manage to pass at the third attempt, but not without going through the greatest agonies of nervousness during the whole process.

However, Angela displayed no such anxieties as she left our house for the second try. Mary and I thought we might go with her, but we realised that our fears might have been transmitted to her, so we stayed home and waited.

We had to do so for a considerable time. Norwich was a journey of about forty-five minutes from home. Roley had taken her early so she could have some practice in city traffic; then there was the time for the test, which would take the best part of an hour; then another forty-five minutes for the home-ward drive. So Angela would probably be away for almost four hours.

Mary and I just could not settle. We watched TV. We did some work in the garden. We listened to records. We were able to concentrate on none of these activities for more than a few minutes. We drank many cups of tea and coffee. But, in spite of all our efforts, we could do nothing to make the time go more quickly. So much depended on the test. Being able to drive herself would make Angela so much more self sufficient.

We spent quite a lot of the intervening period just looking out of the bedroom window. We had gone upstairs because from there we could see so much further up the road.

At long last, the familiar sight of the white Mini Clubman appeared in the road approaching our house. As it got nearer, I could see that the "L" plate was still in position. My heart sank as I imagined just how disappointed our daughter would be at the second failure. As well as helping her to be more independent, a pass would have given her a welcome boost to her self image. Still, we would make every effort to console her. I started to mentally rehearse what I could say to make her feel better.

Mary and I rushed downstairs to meet them. Roley gave us a piece of paper and left. Looking at it I realised it was a pass. Angela had left the learner plates on to play a little joke on us.

She sat down, beaming, and said triumphantly, "I passed, Dad, I *passed!*" I rushed round to the back and front of the car, tearing off the "L" plates, relieved that Angela had a sense of humour. How we hugged and kissed! Our daughter had entered a new phase in her battle for independence.

Chapter 8

WORKING WOMAN

Angela managed to obtain a job as a general office assistant at a small firm based in a village just three miles from our home. She persevered in this highly unsatisfactory position for a number of months. It proved to be unsuitable for her because she couldn't do the many duties required of her in such a tiny place. She couldn't reach files or in fact carry them. She was not able to make the tea, or carry it from one room to another. She could manage a job which could be carried out from a chair, such as typing or using the telephone, but in such a small office a number of miscellaneous duties had to be carried out, and she was not able to cope with many of these because of her physical limitations. She began to suffer from minor illnesses and discomforts such as headaches and colds. I used to try to jolly her along with trite little sayings like, "When the going gets tough, the tough get going". I realise now how silly these were, but, at the time I was so perplexed as to what I could do for the best, that I thought anything I said might be of help to her. Above all, I wanted to ensure that she kept her job. I was so keen to let her have a life that was completely independent of Mary and me.

But Angela's having time off for these minor illnesses, and her inability to deal with the various aspects of the job, culminated with her parting company with the firm by more or less mutual consent. She had made one good, loyal and helpful friend, Joyce, who kept in touch with her for many years after their professional relationship ended. So, Angela's first venture into the world of employment was not entirely without benefit – she had made another friend. In fact, her circle of friends was growing fast, relationships being more easily maintained now that she herself was independently mobile.

One thing that worried Mary and me was what would happen if, when she was out in the car on her own, the car broke down. Around North Norfolk there are many very lonely, narrow lanes. In fact it was not possible to get from our house without travelling several miles along such roads. When she was out, particularly if it was at night, we spent much of the time wondering if she were all right.

The solution to the difficulty came in an unusual and totally unexpected manner. For some time we, as a family had been attending the Baptist Church in Sheringham. Although there was a large congregation, we soon got to know most of the members reasonably well. In conversation with one of these, it was suggested that we got in touch with Securicor who in turn put us in contact with a communications firm, Air Call. When Mary explained our daughter's difficulty, they readily agreed to fit a two way radio set in her car. When we enquired how much this would cost, they told us that all the expense, including the cost of installation, would be met by them.

The generosity of local firms in their gifts towards the provision of the car in the first place, and of this offer from Air Call, was in marked contrast to the meanness of the Department of Health and Social Security. They had turned down Angela's original application for an Invacar, in spite of what was to us, and most other people, a perfectly valid request. By now, these small, unsafe vehicles has been phased out, and instead a Mobility Allowance had been introduced to enable any disabled person who qualified to run their own adapted vehicle. We decided, more in hope than expectation, to apply for this new allowance. To our great surprise, the application was successful, and Angela now had enough money coming in to pay for the upkeep of her vehicle. Also, it was discovered that there was enough money left over from the original car appeal to buy a prefabricated garage. There was no suitable land available at our house, but a kindly local farmer allowed us to erect it just across the road, again without any cost at all. The local Rotaract group provided the concrete for the base and the labour for laying it down.

The two way radio worked like this. If Angela was out in the

car and wanted to contact someone urgently, say in the event
of a breakdown or accident for example, she could call the
communications centre in Norwich on the radio. They would
then call on the ordinary telephone anyone who could help.
So, if Angela was involved in any difficulty, they would call us,
and we would be able to take any action necessary. When this
had been done, Air Call would radio back to Angela to tell her
that Mum or Dad would be with her soon, plus the RAC
mechanic. Air Call told us not only to use the service in dire
emergencies, but for less dramatic events also, such as the fact
that she would be twenty minutes late for tea!

So, one or two major difficulties had been overcome, but the
one that remained seemed likely to be more intractable – the
problem of Angela finding some form of employment. This
seemed very important to me. I wanted her to be self sufficient
in every possible way. Physically, she could manage more in
self care than we would have dreamed possible. But there were
some things she couldn't still manage, like getting in and out of
the bath. Mary and I thought that, in time, perhaps these re-
maining difficulties might be overcome. But the problem of
Angela finding a job remained.

Again, the answer came from a quite unexpected source.
Ever since we had come to live in Norfolk we had taken the
local newspaper, the *Eastern Daily Press*, to keep in touch with
local affairs. Idly looking through it, Mary noticed that the
giant insurance firm, Norwich Union, required home workers
to do typing. We had bought Angela a good electric typewriter
while she was at college, so she could practise at home. She had
become quite proficient in its use, and this seemed like a possible opening for her. Mary rang the Norwich number and
found out that the work would have to be collected from the
Norwich office. We didn't like the idea of Angela having to
drive the twenty-five miles or so into the middle of the busy
city. We couldn't be relied on to go for her because Mary had
a job at the local hospital, and of course I was engaged at the
school all day.

But, during the conversation Mary had with the Norwich
Union employee, the subject of Angela's disabilities cropped

up. It appeared that the firm was trying to keep to the government's rule that all firms over a certain size had to employ a percentage of people who were registered as disabled. It appeared that there might possibly be an opening for Angela.

In due course, an interview was obtained. On the appointed day Mary and our daughter set off for Norwich. I don't think that I felt very hopeful, but they seemed full of confidence. Later that afternoon, the school telephone rang and Mary informed me that Angela had got the job. It was to be in the typing pool, doing audio typing. Whilst this would not make full use of Angela's talents, it would give her life some purpose and point. It would make her feel that she was contributing something to society, as well as giving her some cash in her pocket.

The question which concerned Mary and me was how we could get her to Norwich and back every day. We tried a few advertisements for a lift – we had often seen these – but no help was forthcoming from that quarter. Then I had a thought. She was due to start work on August 1st. The schools broke up during the third week in July, so why couldn't I travel in with her, as a passenger until both she and I felt that she could manage the drive without any supervision? The more we thought about it, the more we thought it might be feasible. In any case, if something was not done soon, Angela would not be able to take the job.

August 1st dawned. Angela had to get up extremely early, round about half past five, in order to get herself ready. Either Mary or I could have helped her to wash and dress, but we were then, as always, trying to make her as self sufficient as she possibly could be.

Angela was very anxious during the drive into the city. There are several very busy roundabouts to be negotiated when approaching from the north, and she went up to each one with much trepidation. I had never travelled into the city with her previously. All such trips had been undertaken by her driving instructor. My trips with her had been confined to a radius of about ten miles from home. But, on this trip, I was very surprised to learn just how competent she was in quite heavy traffic.

We reached the Norwich Union office in a reasonable time. The firm had provided a special parking spot for her quite near one of the entrances. Her office was on one of the upper floors and as she couldn't climb the stairs, she would have to do what most of the other people did – use the lift. The problem here was that she couldn't reach the lift buttons. This was solved by the commissionaires. They arranged themselves into a rota, so that each morning and evening one of them was on hand to take Angela up or down. Naturally, very often one of the girls in the pool would be at the lift at the same time as she was, so the services of a commissionaire could be dispensed with. But this was just one of the ways in which the management and staff went out of their way to make things as easy as possible for her.

While she was in the office I spent the time around Norwich. I got to know quite a bit about the city and used up many hours in the fine library. I continued to do this for a week, and on the Friday, on the way home, Angela said, "You know, Dad, I'm sure I feel confident enough to drive to work on my own now. You don't have to come in with me any more!"

I had been prepared to spend the whole of the summer holiday travelling to Norwich with her, but I had been impressed with the standard of her driving, and also with the confidence she displayed in traffic.

"All right. If you still feel the same way on Monday morning you can go on your own. But remember, I'll come in with you for as long as you like – well, at least for the next four weeks."

To tell the truth, I had rather enjoyed the week. Apart from the visits to the library and the many historic buildings, I realised that just by being with her, it saved Mary and me many anxious hours wondering if she would be all right on her daily journey. I really thought that by the Monday morning her confidence would have evaporated and I would be renewing my acquaintance with Norfolk's premier city.

However, when the Monday dawned, I was surprised to hear that she was still determined to go it alone, and it seemed no time at all before she was all ready to go. The reversing out of the garage was a quite dangerous operation for anyone, because although there wasn't a lot of traffic about, the roads around the school are very narrow, and the school and house are on a very nasty corner. So, Mary and I watched her back out of the garage, pull forward, turn right and disappear into the distance. We were left wondering if she would be safe, and whether it wouldn't have been better after all if I had continued to accompany her to work at least for a little more time. We had another cup of coffee, and waited in the living room. We knew that it should take her about forty-five minutes, if nothing went wrong. Of course, during the waiting time we imagined all the things that could happen. I think our thoughts covered the whole range of mishaps from a fatal crash to gearbox failure.

As the estimated time of Angela's arrival in Norwich drew near, our anxieties increased. Forty-six, forty-seven minutes had gone by when our silence was interrupted by the strident ring of the telephone. It was her. In fact, she told us, she had been at the office for about ten minutes, but for some reason she couldn't get through. Yes, she was fine. No, she hadn't had any difficulties or near misses. In fact, everything was hunky-dory, in the phrase that was popular in the Powell household at the time.

Angela's time at Norwich Union was very satisfactory from everyone's point of view. She was very happy there. The work was well within her capability. She was glad that she had something useful to do, for which she was being paid a reasonable salary. We were pleased that it gave her a start in a career that would be rewarding. And we soon got over our anxieties about her driving. The main reason for our renewed confidence was the fact that we knew that if anything did go wrong, Air Call would be in touch. She made many good friends at work, and quite often would invite one of them home for the weekend.

At about this time I had the idea of writing a book. I wanted the world to know what a struggle life had been for Angela, and how well she had met the challenges of her life, challenges that most people would know nothing about. I thought that she might object to readers knowing all the intimate parts of her life, but the reverse was true. She seemed to be all for it. As my typing was very erratic, I would write out a few pages in longhand, and she would type it for me. In this way the first three chapters of the book were written. But then, because of pressure of work and the pain of reliving past traumas, the book was forgotten, and for several years the partly finished manuscript languished at the bottom of a sideboard drawer.

This was a time too when she began to experiment with her name. She had been christened Angela Mary Linda. Angela, because we liked it. Mary, after her mother. And Linda, after Mary's niece. I always referred to her as Angela, but Mary and Paul and others tended to shorten it to "Angie" or even just "Anj". She tried several spellings, such as "Anghi", "Anji" and other variations on this theme. But the one she finally settled on was "Angi" and this is how most of the people who knew her began to spell her name.

Now that she was in her late teens, she was faced with problems of a different nature. Because she was so badly disabled, and she appreciated just how badly, she was very anxious that her development in those areas which were not obviously affected was "normal". She was particularly keen to know that her sexual development was satisfactory. For instance, she showed great interest in the development of her breasts, which started at the usual time. For a while she had been very disappointed with her "gnat bites" as she called them, but she soon "filled out". Then, she was very pleased when her periods started, again at about the same age that her schoolmates started.

These increases in maturity inevitably led to talk about boy friends, marriage and babies. She had seen how interested Mary was in family life and children, and I think Angela inherited some of this maternalistic tendency from her mother. In fact if our second child had been "normal", I imagine we would have had several more, but as it was we had decided that we had better stop at two, and I underwent a vasectomy. But now, at the dawn of adulthood, Angela was subject to the same desires and yearnings that any girl of nineteen would have to contend with.

The dilemma for Mary and me could be stated like this.

Until Angela was about seventeen years old we had been able to solve most of her problems for her. If she wanted to go to a pop concert, I took her. If she had an unexpected personal or medical difficulty, Mary dealt with it. So, we were able to enter into the private life of our daughter in a way that would not have been possible, nor even desirable, if she had not been disabled. But now we were entering into quite unknown territory and we didn't know how to handle it. There seemed very little we could do. We just had to stand by and watch Angela's friends have boy friends, get married and have babies.

At my suggestion, Mary and I decided on a strategy to protect Angela from too much disappointment. Any time the subject cropped up we would make a comment like, "Well, don't forget, not everyone gets married. Look at Janice, for example, she's single and leads a perfectly happy life."

Or perhaps, "Many married couples are wretchedly unhappy. And think about how many marriages end in divorce."

We hoped in this way to steer Angela's thinking to the idea that marriage was not the supreme happiness that many young women fantasised it was. But, in spite of all our well intentioned efforts to protect her, it became obvious from her reading, her conversation and the efforts she undertook to make herself look as attractive as possible, that she still nurtured the dream.

Because she lived a sheltered life, most of the people she mixed with were women. True, there were a few opportunities for meeting the opposite sex, but these were strictly limited. So, one day, Angela decided to do something about it.

CHAPTER 9

H.

Mary and I had always encouraged Angela to be as independent as she possibly could. I think we were always vaguely aware that we would not always be around to be of assistance. This independence extended to her correspondence. However, it became apparent that she was receiving many more letters than she had been previously. One day, she volunteered the information that she had joined the Christian Friendship Fellowship, based at Doncaster. She told us that she had written to several young men and they had all replied. It soon became apparent that these letters would eventually lead to meetings. Some of the boys visited our house, and we took Angela to visit others. None of these relationships lasted, and the letters ceased.

One of the correspondents, however, one Hartley Graham, persisted in his letters. It became a family joke. He lived in North Shields, and when a letter appeared on our door mat with this postmark, either Mary or I would say, "There's another letter from Hartley Hare. Perhaps we'll see him hopping over the fields at any moment." This was a reference to a current children's television programme, in which the main character was Hartley. She would usually let us read Hartley's letters. She often said that she wished that he would stop writing, as he was, she said, "too religious".

She received one of his letters, and before she had finished reading it, exclaimed, "What do you think? He's coming to the UEA!"

This is the University of East Anglia, situated in Norwich.

"Well, that's a coincidence. Fancy him coming to live that near. Anyway, you'll be able to meet him at last," Mary put in quickly.

"No fear. I've told you before. He's far too religious for me. I didn't mind too much writing to him, but I certainly don't want to meet him."

"But, he's only going to be twenty odd miles away. He'll be away from home and friends, and could probably do with some company," Mary countered.

I listened to this conversation with quiet amusement but no comment. But it was obvious that our daughter had absolutely no intention of being railroaded into this relationship. Perhaps she was afraid he would be disappointed to find that she was so badly handicapped – but this hadn't deterred her from meeting the others. Maybe he really was too religious for her. For whatever reason, she seemed determined that the postal friendship should not develop into something more personal.

The episode culminated in Angela's final riposte.

"Well, if you do invite him here, I shall go out."

And she meant it too.

They continued writing to one another, without meeting, in spite of the fact that they were both in Norwich during the working day. But Angela still didn't relish a meeting.

Then, quite out of the blue, things came to a head. Angela came home from work one day in a very excitable state. As soon as she came through the front door, she said,

"Now, I want you both to sit down. You'll never guess who I've seen today – Hartley. And he's lovely!"

She went on to tell us that he had met her as she was coming out of the office.

"And, what do you think? He gave me a beautiful bunch of flowers. They're in the car."

She couldn't manage to carry them in, of course, as she had her handbag in one hand and her walking stick in the other. I rushed across the road to get them, and found that they were indeed beautiful. It was the first time that a member of the opposite sex had given her flowers. They met a few times in Norwich, and it became clear that Hartley was having difficulties. There were severe family problems, and this was affecting his studies adversely. He had decided to drop out and live in a bedsit in a not very salubrious district in Norwich. He was desperately unhappy, and was beginning to find in Angela the emotional support that he was unable to get from his own family.

After a few weeks Angela asked us if she might invite him home for the weekend. We had been invited to a christening in the church just a hundred yards from home, so it seemed a good opportunity to introduce him to our friends, and to the rest of the family.

I think it would be true to say that we were shocked by his appearance. He was about five feet four in height, and quite slim and muscular. But his clothes! He had on a pair of trainers with holes in them. His trousers had holes in the knees. But, when we got beyond his lack of sartorial elegance, we found that he was a caring, decent lad. Obviously, he was not a very happy young man, but the weekend passed pleasantly for us all, including the christening. Mary and I had previously decided that he was Angela's friend, and that people would have to accept him as he was.

He soon left the bedsit, and went to live in the YMCA in Norwich. Soon he was coming home with Angela and staying nights in our house. He started to stay weekends with us too. He occasionally helped me with the tough physical chores around the house – he was far fitter and stronger than I. Soon it became obvious that it would be better for him to leave his bedsit and come and live permanently with us. We had a spare room, and the arrangement suited Angela perfectly.

We found that the DHSS behaved rather oddly in respect to Hartley's change of address. Whilst he was at the YMCA, and during the time he was at his bedsit, his rent was paid. But when he came to live with us, they refused to pay him anything towards his rent. The excuse was that he was now living with his "family".

It was getting to be obvious by now that Angela and Hartley were becoming more than just good friends. But it still came as a big surprise when, after tea one evening, he said, "Eddie, could I see you on your own for a moment?"

I know it might seem that I was unobservant and insensitive, but for the life of me I couldn't begin to think what he wanted to see me about. All manner of thoughts crowded into my brain in the space of a few seconds. I led him into the adjoining room. We stood, looking out of the window into the garden, and it was obvious that he was going to have a struggle to say whatever was on his mind. But, after a few moments, I broke the ice.

"All right, H., shoot!"

Our son, Paul, had started to call him H., and it seemed to stick.

Making a visible effort to control himself, he managed to stammer, "Angela and I would like to get married."

He turned away, as if the effort had been too much for him. Perhaps he feared my answer would be in the negative. But, I thought, would he be good enough for my only daughter? I felt a bit faint, and sat down.

"Well, H., I must say this has come as a bit of a shock. I expect you've talked it over with Angela, and she's in agreement with it."

Again he nodded. He was a man of few words. I told him about all the difficulties he would face. Angela could never cope with any housework, except of the simplest sort. There could never be any question of children, as the local doctor had indicated that although it was possible for Angela to conceive, the shape of her body would make it extremely hazardous for her to carry a child.

"I am genuinely in love with her, and Angela and I have talked things over at great length. I'm sure all these difficulties can be overcome."

From the sincerity in his voice, I was sure too.

"There's just one other problem."

His eyes narrowed. A frown of disappointment crossed his face.

"Where do you propose to live? You would be welcome to stay with us – there's plenty of room – but I think it would be much better if you could find a place of your own."

"But, apart from that, you have no objection?"

I smiled at him. He'd make a good husband and son-in-law.

"Tell you what. As soon as you've got somewhere to live,

Mary and I will give you all the support we can. Welcome to the family."

We rushed in to tell the two ladies the result of our discussion. Angela and Hartley became engaged on December 1st 1982. They wanted to get married in about six months.

On superficial consideration, Hartley may not have seemed to be much of a "catch" for a well loved daughter. He was unemployed, a university failure and with very little prospects of following a worthwhile career. But he was genuinely looking for a job, and was prepared to have a go at almost anything. Angela was still holding down her job at Norwich Union, so at least there would be one reasonable income coming in. In view of this, I spent some time with him attempting to persuade him to try and resume his studies, but he would have none of this. He and I had established a good relationship, and I think he would have done almost anything for me, with just one exception. He would not have anything to do with any form of further education. It was about the only subject that we ever had words about, and after a while I could see that further discussion might lead to disagreement, so I never mentioned it again.

But Hartley did have much in his favour. He had a kindly nature, was physically strong (quite important for dealing with Angela), seemed to accept Mary and me more as parents than prospective parents-in-law and, most of all, was obviously very fond of our daughter, as she was of him. He also accepted her physical limitations and the extra burdens these would place on him after they were married. After all, he had lived as one of the family for some time and had first-hand knowledge of his future wife's needs. So, after some time, we were able to accept him as a prospective son-in-law, and as someone who would be able to give Angela the continuing support that she needed. In short, Mary and I felt that we could trust our daughter to Hartley's care. This was very important, as the constant worry of the parents of handicapped children is, "What will happen to our child when we are no longer able to help her?" No matter how caring the parents, this time will inevitably come, either through infirmity or death. As parents, we couldn't bear to think of our precious girl having to enter an institution because she wasn't entirely self-sufficient. All in all, we felt that Hartley would not only be a good husband, but also a considerate carer. He was also determined not to expose Angela to any risk of conception, and had a vasectomy.

In fact, Hartley was keeping himself occupied with a variety of temporary jobs. He seemed to be very content with any venture that called for physical endeavour. One of these was as a labourer on a building site – he was very happy there. Around the house, he was on hand with any heavy lifting.

As soon as marriage had been decided on, Mary went into flurries of activity. I'm fairly sure that no one could imagine the amount of effort she put in during the next few months to make sure that everything possible was done to make the day one to remember. The tentative date of June 12th was made, and as it was now early January I wondered how much more frantic my wife's activities would get as the big day got nearer. Up to this time, it had not been established where the couple would live. They put their names down on the local council list, and I supposed that if all else failed they could always live with us. After all, we'd be using one bedroom less.

Angela had been receiving the "Old Boys'" magazine from Gresham's. In one of the issues, the headmaster wrote that he was somewhat disappointed the school chapel was only very rarely used for weddings. We all thought it would be wonderful if the wedding could take place there. We had attended various functions at the chapel, and the pews face inward rather than to the front. Now the chapel at the school is not licensed for weddings, so a special license had to be obtained. This involved several clerical gentlemen, including the Archbishop of Canterbury. The licence turned out to be a very impressive document indeed.

Throughout the spring of 1982 Mary's frenzied activity continued with much acceleration. Soon, everything seemed to be in place, at least as far as any human action can make it so. The chapel was booked, the licence obtained. The reception was to be held at the local Community Centre, in Holt. A horse and carriage were to take the couple from the chapel to the reception. But the question of who was to officiate had not been settled.

We had a conference, and it was decided to ask Ian Pusey, the Rector of Bletchley, Buckinghamshire. We had known Ian and his wife Ros for many years. He had been instrumental in convincing me that I ought to be confirmed in the Church of England when he was a curate at Waltham Abbey. He had also married our son Paul, and Gill. We telephoned him, and were all delighted when Ian said he would be able to do it.

The final arrangements were these. The bridesmaids were Nicola, our granddaughter, and Sally, one of Angela's friends who lived in our village. Christopher, our grandson, was delighted to be pageboy. Paul and Gill were ushers and one of Hartley's friends, Ian Terry, was to be the best man.

About a month prior to the wedding we were all due to attend the wedding, in Southampton, of Gill's sister, Sue. On the Sunday before this, Hartley complained of severe stomach pains. As he was not prone to illness, nor was he a complaining sort of person, Mary treated his sickness with seriousness and we took him to the local hospital in Cromer where appendicitis was diagnosed. The next day an operation was performed and on the Wednesday he was back home with us. Mary and I were convinced that we would have to cancel the weekend trip to Southampton, but Hartley would not hear of it. So, on Friday, Angela, Hartley, Mary and myself set out for the south. The weekend went very well, with Hartley not suffering any ill effects. This said much for his toughness and durability, qualities which I much admire in anyone.

By the beginning of June, all the arrangements had been made, checked and re-checked. I had had very little to do with this, except when it came to the making out of the cheques. But this was to be one occasion when I did not mind what expense was incurred, although I couldn't have done it without the co-operation of my bank manager. I have nothing but admiration for the way Mary took the responsibility for seeing that everything went smoothly, which it did.

Nothing had been heard from the Council regarding any housing for the couple. Even in such a sparsely populated area as North Norfolk, the demands on the local authority's housing department are immense, and I was not too confident about our daughter's application. Secretly too, I think I may have been hoping, rather selfishly, that maybe it would be as well if they didn't get a house of their own. This would enable me to keep an eye on them! However, my wishes were not to be realised. A very short while before the wedding a Council official rang up and asked to speak to Angela. When she had finished listening she put down the telephone and turned to the rest of us, her eyes shining with excitement and joy.

"You'll never guess what that was all about."

We all indeed had been trying to make head or tail of the conversation, but as most of the speaking had been done from the person at the Council Office, we had not succeeded in making much sense of the dialogue.

"They've given us a bungalow in Holt. It's only got one bedroom, but at least we will have somewhere on our own."

In spite of my feelings, I could not help but rejoice with them. And Holt is only three miles from where we lived.

It turned out that as 1982 had been designated as the Year of the Disabled, the Housing Committee had decided to make a house available to a handicapped person, and Angela and Hartley had been the lucky recipients.

Soon, the allocation was confirmed by letter. We made a trip to Holt to see it, but found that construction had only just begun. But the site was a very pleasant one and no doubt it would be quite suitable for the young couple. They were so excited to think that they now would be able to set up home on their own, to be able to come and go as they pleased, and to be able to invite friends in for meals. Even I had to admit to myself that this was the better solution. Mary and I too, would have time on our own, although we had not thought about this too often.

Chapter 10

MARRIAGE

As with any long awaited and anticipated event, the last week before the wedding seemed to go very slowly in spite of all the work involved for Mary and me. My private thoughts about it varied from hour to hour. At any given time, I would be rejoicing that Angela had achieved another life goal. A short time later, I would be anxious in case Angela was doing the wrong thing. I guess I just didn't want to lose her. To the outsider, it would have seemed that Angela was very much dependent upon her parents, but the truth of the matter was that the dependence was a two way affair. Already there had been a snag with the bungalow. It would not be ready for occupation until a few weeks after the wedding. Until it was ready they would live with us.

Saturday, June 12th 1982 dawned very early for the Powell household. Assorted friends visited with their good wishes. The flowers were delivered, and soon it was time to get ready. The house seemed full of bridesmaids, bouquets and buttonholes. Everyone had new clothes and at one point I began to wonder seriously if I had acted wisely in buying a complete new rig-out. The suit was fine. I had already tried it on several times. But the lovely new white shirt was a different matter entirely. It looked exquisite in the box, all pristine and creaseless. When I tried it on however, I discovered that it was a "slimfit". I had attempted to lose weight prior to this day, but when I put on the shirt I found it would only just button up. Still, my waistcoat would fasten and it hid the slight pull of the shirt across the chest, and nobody except myself would be any the wiser. My freedom of movement was, however, severely restricted and I would have to put up with this throughout a long and stressful day.

Minor difficulties like this apart, the morning went well. No-one felt hungry so we dispensed with lunch. The cars for the bridesmaids and other guests arrived and went, and all of a sudden the house was quiet, the only occupants being my daughter and me. We sat on the settee and held hands. I think we were both near to tears. She had lived with us for over twenty years, and during that period the only time she had ever spent away from home at night, apart from the hospital stays, was when she went to a Guide camp, and this was only for two nights. Sitting there, not saying much, we were lost in our own private thoughts. What would the future hold for the young couple?

We were both still in our own private worlds when the doorbell rang. I think we both felt like two people about to make their first parachute jump. We didn't actually shout "Geronimo", but we felt like it. During the short car journey we didn't say much, but looking at my daughter in her white wedding outfit I couldn't help thinking how beautiful she was. Her walking stick had been decorated with white ribbon to match the rest of the outfit. The big white car rumbled along at a slow pace and I wasn't really aware of where we were. Soon the gates of the school were directly on our left, and the car swung in through them.

As we wound through the school grounds, we passed the cricket pitches. There was a game in progress but the boys stopped playing for a moment, and waved their caps at us. Soon, the car stopped outside the chapel.

"This is it!" I thought. "Too late to change their minds now!"

Angela was rather anxious to get out of the car as elegantly as she possibly could. This was not an easy thing to do. However, with much concentration, and a little help from me, she managed it. We were almost at the chapel door, when she suddenly stopped and cried out, "Help, I've forgotten my bouquet! It must still be in the car."

The bouquet was retrieved by Paul, and we progressed, very slowly.

On entering the chapel, we were amazed at the large crowd

of people there. We had invited over two hundred guests, but there were many more than that number seated. The aisle seemed a mile long, and I wondered how Angela would manage it. We had previously discussed the possibility of my taking her down in her wheelchair, but she had insisted on walking down the aisle, "like a proper bride". Ian, who of course preceded us, stopped at various intervals to allow us to catch up. We moved at a very slow pace, and my thoughts turned again to the question of my daughter's courage and persistence. How much easier it would have been with the wheelchair.

We had had a rehearsal, but we had not practised the walk. When we arrived at the altar, Ian gave us a few minutes for Angela to catch her breath, and the service began. Because of the number of people there, the hymns sounded stupendous. From time to time I stole a glance at Angela, and she looked radiant. I know that this adjective is often applied to brides, but this is about the best word to describe her face on that day. The proceedings were interrupted a few times by tremendously loud claps of thunder, and we could hear heavy rain on the roof. I imagined that every one was thinking what a shame it was after such a lovely start, and was praying for it to clear up by the end of the service. It did, and although the roads were wet, the couple were able to travel to the reception in the open horse-drawn carriage, as planned. I was very moved to see Hartley lifting Angela up on to the carriage.

Slowly, the congregation, or rather those who had been invited to the reception, made their way to the Community Centre, about a mile from the school. Because of the storm the electricity had been cut off, so the caterers had the job of keeping the meal hot. And how were we going to see? They decided to go into the town and buy some candles, so the tables were all set up with candles on them when we got there. This was an excellent way for all the guests to get into conversation. I don't know how the meal was kept warm, but it was delicious, and all the more romantic by candle light.

The reception continued in much the same way as many others that I had attended, and soon Angela and Hartley were

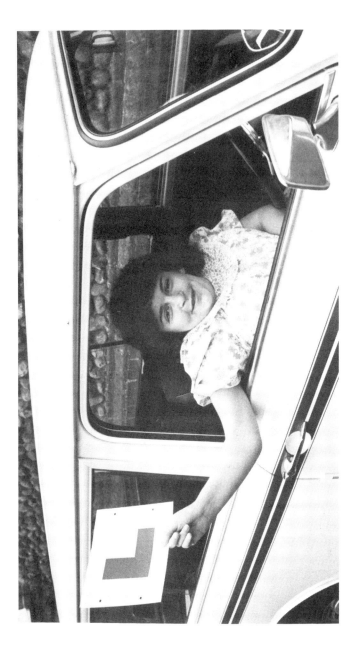

on the way to their honeymoon. They weren't going far – Hartley had only just started a new job and didn't like to take time off. The honeymoon consisted of a few days at the Manor Hotel, Mundesley, about fourteen miles away.

Before the reception broke up, one of our longstanding friends, Marjorie Harvey, had asked everyone at the reception to sign a tablecloth. Then she took it home and embroidered all the signatures, using a variety of coloured threads. The result was very pleasing, and a potent reminder of the big day. We still use this cloth on special occasions.

Mary and I had dined in the Manor on a number of occasions, and during the honeymoon we decided to surprise the happy couple by turning up for dinner one evening. We had been wondering how they were getting on, and we had a delightful evening with our daughter and son-in-law.

After their brief honeymoon, they returned to our house to live. Naturally, they couldn't wait to get into their own place, but they made the best of things. Mary and I rather enjoyed their company, and we experienced a number of delightful evening outings to various places of entertainment. In particular, we very much appreciated the Little Theatre in Sheringham. Here, they have numerous amateur dramatic productions each year, and these are of a very high standard indeed. We got to know many of the artistes and this added to our pleasure. Because of her short stature, Angela couldn't see unless she sat in the front row, and so we had to get used to sitting there, even if it did mean getting a cricked neck. As it happens, Mary and I became so used to being on the front row that this is where we chose to sit even when Angela was not there with us.

One morning about four weeks after the wedding, Angela felt quite unwell and decided not to go to work. We knew she must be ill, otherwise she would not want to stay home. She often felt like this, and we thought that a day's rest at home with a little pampering from mum might put her right in a short time. By this time Hartley had got a job at a hardware shop in a nearby town, and so mother and daughter were able to spend the day without interference from husbands. She went to bed early. In the evening, some friends came around to see the video of the wedding, but as Angela had already seen it a couple of times she decided not to come down. Half way through the video Mary made a cup of tea. Tea was about the only drink that Angela really liked, and so Mary took a cup upstairs. I became aware that Mary was shouting in an agitated fashion.

"Eddie, come up quickly."

I made my way to the bedroom as quickly as my legs could carry me.

"I can't seem to wake her."

I tried to do so but no amount of shaking and talking to her could arouse her. We couldn't think of what could possibly be wrong, so we had no alternative but to telephone for the doctor. Because Angela was well known at the Health Centre, and because the doctors all realised how delicately balanced Angela's health always was, there was no problem about a house call. The doctor examined her thoroughly, but could not make a diagnosis. He decided to give her an injection of something or other, and this did have the effect of waking her up. The doctor promised to return in the morning. Angela slept until then.

When the doctor returned, he was not satisfied that he had done his best for her, so he telephoned the West Norfolk Hospital in Norwich in the hope that they would be able to find out what was wrong. She stayed there for three days, undergoing tests, but still they were unable to find the cause of her distress, and she continued to be very poorly indeed. The doctors there came to the conclusion that they would not be able to help her, and as her condition continued to deteriorate, the only course that seemed sensible was to send her where she might be helped. This turned out to be Addenbrooke's Hospital, Cambridge. This has an enviable reputation in the treatment of obscure and difficult medical conditions, particularly those concerning the central nervous system. Mary was at the West Norfolk when this decision was made, and so went in the ambulance with her. Mary telephoned me at school, and I immediately informed my Area Education Officer, a very kind and understanding friend who knew Angela and Mary quite well. He suggested that I have as much time off as I needed, to go to Cambridge and support Mary and our daughter. As it was only two weeks before the end of the summer term, and as there were so many things to do at this time, I was in somewhat of a dilemma. How was the school going to be able to manage without me? In the event, the staff told me that they could manage perfectly well, and I never had any false ideas of my own indispensibility after that.

Mary described the journey from Norwich to Addenbrooke's as "horrendous". The trip was made with the siren sounding, and somehow the driver had arranged with the police for all the traffic lights to be in their favour. As for me, our car was in Norwich, as Mary had driven it to visit Angela. Paul, our son, drove me to pick it up, and I was able to drive to Cambridge and my wife and daughter.

I think it would be a gross understatement to write that Mary was pleased to see me. She was also delighted to learn that I would be able to stay there for as long as it took. We couldn't be accommodated in the hospital, so we arranged to stay in a bed and breakfast establishment nearby. We were able to obtain a special ticket to enable us to eat in the staff restaurant, where the prices were low and so was the quality of the food.

We had an anxious few days whilst various medical checks and procedures were being carried out. Even with all the sophisticated equipment and the undoubted skill of the staff, the cause of Angela's distress could not be discovered with any certainty. The best hypothesis was that maybe the valve wasn't working properly. So we gave our consent, in the absence of her husband, to an operation to replace the valve. It was to be done the following day. Although Mary and I had given permission for the operation, we were by no means happy about it. We remembered how desperately ill Angela had been when the original valve had been inserted. Perhaps, we thought, now that she's older and a lot stronger it would not prove to be as dangerous.

Angela felt and looked gravely ill. During the evening prior to the operation she asked the question that we didn't want to answer, because we didn't know how.

"Mum, I'm not going to die am I?"

For a moment Mary and I were stunned into silence. The fear on our daughter's face was plain to see. I spoke first.

"We all have to die sometime, sweetheart, but you'll be all right this time."

I hoped that my voice imparted the confidence which I did not feel. Mary put her arms around the small young body and said, "You are going to be fine, darling. I know you're tired but your dad and I will stay with you until you are fast asleep, and we'll be up to see you before you have the operation."

This reply seemed to put her mind at rest. Actually, the thought of the operation didn't seem to bother her too much, and she soon drifted off to sleep.

The next day was Friday, and Paul had arranged to bring Hartley to Cambridge to join us for the weekend. The woman who owned the bed and breakfast establishment was full up, but agreed to put up two camp beds in our bedroom, if that was suitable to us. It wasn't a very satisfactory arrangement but it seemed better than having the two sleep somewhere else.

For most of the time Mary and I sat at her bedside. Occasionally she would wake up, and seeing us there gave her a lot of confidence and peace of mind. If she seemed to be in a rather deep sleep, we would slip down to the dining room for a meal. It may seem odd, but worry has always given me a good appetite, whilst most other people I know have the opposite reaction. Some time each day we spent in the little chapel, in quiet thought and prayer. The latter was quite difficult for us – we were just too miserable, but we knew that the people at our Christian Fellowship back home in Cromer were holding us up before God, and we really were conscious of their support in this way. Also they sent us quite a large cheque to help with our expenses which were now considerable, and we were very grateful for this too. When we had filled in the admission form, in the line where "Religion" was to be entered, we had written simply "Christian". The result was that we had bedside visits from the ministers of all the major Christian denominations. Thus we were never short of people praying for us.

We were surprised when, a few days later, we were told that she could be taken home. To us, she seemed very unwell and was sleeping for most of the time. We thought that a longer stay at the hospital would be best, although of course, we badly wanted her to be well enough to be discharged. We wondered if we could give her the sort of care she needed. But the doctors assured us that she was well enough to leave the hospital. They loaned us a couple of pillows, and we made her as comfortable as we could on the back seat of the car. Very careful driving made it possible for Angela to sleep for most of the two-hour journey, and Mary and I were very relieved when we arrived in Baconsthorpe. Soon Angela was in her own bed and with her husband.

The next day was Monday and she was still drowsy for most of the time. I just couldn't leave her bedside, and Mary spent most of the day there with me. Hartley was in the shop for the working day, and Mary spent much time over the household chores. As I kept my vigil, I continued to speculate on the wisdom of her discharge from hospital. She looked so ill, and only occasionally regaining full consciousness. During one of her short, lucid periods she looked up at me and said, "Don't worry, Dad, I'm not scared of dying now."

I had to fight hard to keep back the tears, but I managed to say, "That's OK, sweetheart, but I'm sure you aren't going to die for a long time yet."

She drifted back to sleep, and I wondered if indeed her time had come. Then I remembered the biblical story of Elijah who had stretched himself over the son of a widow, and the boy, who had been desperately ill was restored to health. It occurred to me that I ought to do the same thing to my daughter. So I did this, seven times. I know now that Elijah stretched himself three times, but I didn't remember the details of the story too well at the time. Paul, who worked in the local council offices, didn't feel he could leave her either so he stayed with us all that day. He and Mary came up to the bedroom from time to time, but for some reason I just could not leave, although Angela was asleep or in some sort of minor coma. I think I spent most of that day in tears. At one point Paul came up and asked, "Are you all right, Dad?"

I was having one of my more violent bouts of crying at the time.

"Yes, I'll be OK, Paul. I just need to be here with her."

The next day she was no better, and the doctor was sent for. He, of course, was very familiar with Angela's medical history, having been responsible for her health care for seven years. Another immediate admission to hospital was indicated, this time to the Norfolk and Norwich.

By this time, the new term had started, and I did not feel that I could ask for more time off, in view of the generous way I had been treated by the local authority at the end of the previous term. So Mary had to go in the ambulance without my support. I didn't like to handle the situation in this way, but there seemed very little that could be done about it. As Paul and I saw the two into the ambulance, I heard Paul say quietly to his mother, "Try not to worry too much, Mum. God won't give you more than you can cope with."

This remark appeared to give Mary new hope. Paul and I watched the ambulance disappear with our two precious women inside.

I made the journey to Norwich as soon as school had finished for the day, and learned that Angela was to be transferred to Addenbrooke's the next day.

In the morning, as soon as it was practicable, I telephoned the Area Office, and was given permission by the Area Officer to have a few weeks compassionate leave. I knew that, whatever the consequences, I just could not leave Mary to cope with the next period of our lives without my help. In the event the granting of some leave with pay went through without any hitch. That took a great load off my mind. I knew several excellent supply teachers, and the employment of one of these during my absence meant that the school would function quite well without me. I telephoned most days to check up, to answer queries and to give advice.

When we arrived at Addenbrooke's, we found that we were

able to be accommodated in the hospital. We were glad of this because we were so much closer to Angela all the time. This time, no operation was suggested, just careful looking after and monitoring. The doctors just didn't seem to be able to find out what was wrong. To be fair to the medical staff, there were so many malfunctions in Angela's body that her present difficulties could have been due to any one of these.

After about ten days, she was very much better, and she was able to be discharged. This time Mary and I were in full agreement. Our daughter seemed so much better. The improvement continued at home, and shortly she was fit enough to get out of bed for short periods. Soon she was up all day, and she tried to walk. She found this a bit tricky, and we had to give her a lot of encouragement. Eventually she was as fit as she had been before her last bout of illness. Unfortunately none of us felt that she would be well enough to work, and she resigned from her job at Norwich Union. She was however, able to drive again, which gave her a great sense of freedom. Hartley had also lost his job because of his frequent absences. His employer had not been at all sympathetic during this trying time. They were still living with us in Baconsthorpe, but one day the news came through that the bungalow in Holt was now ready, and so Mary and I had to brace ourselves for what seemed to us to be our first real separation from our beloved daughter.

CHAPTER 11

DETERIORATION

All too soon they moved out. The three miles to Holt seemed to be much further. I could hardly grasp the fact that a completely new era had started for Mary and me. No longer were we a family of three, but we had now been reduced to two.

Angela seemed to cope with her new status and address better than her mother and father did. She quickly adapted to her new lifestyle, and took great delight in doing what she could around the bungalow. Hartley did most of the housework, during the periods when he was not working. When he was in employment, Paul's wife Gill did some of the housework. Even so, there was a great deal for Hartley to do, and he made a marvellous job of looking after the home and his wife. It seemed to us and our friends that the arrangements that Angela and Hartley were forced to make worked quite well for them. They both appeared to be satisfied with the scheme they had worked out.

Hartley did manage to find some temporary employment from time to time, and Angela was able to obtain a few months' work at a local charity. But their earnings did not amount to much, and for most of their married life they were both unemployed. But they were financially independent, and on the few occasions that they had to borrow some small sums of money from us, they made every effort to repay. The marriage seemed to be successful, and certainly both were very happy.

As the months passed, it became clear that Angela's general health was deteriorating. There was nothing specific, but she seemed to be in many rather indefinite ways less active, less confident and certainly less buoyant each time we saw her, which was quite often. She had always been a rather emotional person, as is her mother, but at this time in her life she began to suffer from minor bouts of depression. I think now that these were due to her increasing physical difficulties. With hindsight, it seems that neither Mary nor I could bring ourselves to acknowledge Angela's physical deterioration. We were afraid to acknowledge the facts even though they were staring us in the face.

At one point Angela decided that she and her husband could do with a break from each other. So she came to stay with us for a week. She stayed two days, which were punctuated by numerous telephone calls to and from Hartley. One incident which occurred during this short stay with us illustrates the indomitable spirit of our daughter, and her sense of humour. On the first evening with us, she decided to get undressed downstairs. She had some difficulty undoing the buttons at the back of her dress so I helped. When the dress had finally been removed, she turned to me and smilingly said, "I'll bet it's a long time since you helped to undress a twenty-five year old woman, Dad!"

The two of us laughed more heartily than we had done for a long time.

She returned home and settled down again to her own domestic life with Hartley. They entertained us and other people to meals, but of course Hartley did the bulk of the preparation. Angela did what she could. As a wedding gift, the Cromer Christian Fellowship, of which the whole family were now members, gave her a most beautifully made tea trolley on castors. This had been made by one of the members, Mike Barker. When we were invited to tea, they loaded the trolley with food and Angela would proudly wheel the trolley into the living room.

By now the Mini Clubman was showing signs of its age. It had proved extremely reliable and had never let her down, but small areas of rust began to show and it was obvious that a new car was going to be needed. I felt so bad about the fact that there was so little I could do to help.

The numbers of pupils at Baconsthorpe School had declined to the point where the local education authority, in conjunction with the Norwich Diocesan Council for Education, had decided to close it. There were of course the usual protests from the local residents, but closure came. I was fortunate in that during the last term I obtained another headship at Blakeney Primary School, to start in the September. But we were living in the School House, and we would have to find alternative accommodation. I made several impassioned pleas to the church authorities, but to no avail. Similar appeals were made to the council housing authority, with the same result. Apparently, we had no chance of a council house because we were not old, had no children and were not looking after a disabled person. If Angela had still been living with us, the council may well have been able to help. The only alternative was to purchase a house, and I did not think that at the age of fifty-four any building society would be willing to grant me a mortgage. Even if they did, I doubted if I would be able to keep up the repayments.

In spite of these reservations, we ardently scanned the estate agents' windows and the local newspapers for possible answers to our housing difficulty. I wrote "we" but really it was Mary who did all the leg work. I only went to visit the potential new homes as a sort of second opinion. Eventually we found a suitable property, agreed with the owner on a price, and applied for a mortgage. To my astonishment the mortgage was granted and we moved in. All of my savings, which did not amount to a great deal, went as a deposit. When I received the documentation back from the building society, I realised that the repayments were horrendously high. As each month passed, and the payments were made, I breathed a sigh of relief. But the cost of living plus the repayments meant that each month we had little to spare.

Thus I felt very hurt and disappointed that there was no way that I could help solve Angela's car problem. The answer came in an unexpected and miraculous way.

Our near neighbours at this time, Joan and Mike Wylie, have a son Jonathan, who is disabled with cerebral palsy. He and Angela were about the same age. Jon had been offered a citizens' band radio by the local Lions club. He had declined the gift because he already had one, from which he had gained a lot of pleasure. The representative of the club asked if he knew any other disabled person who might be interested in receiving it. Jon gave Angela's name, and the CB was to be installed in her car. She felt this was the most beneficial way to use it, as it meant she could summon help if her Mini broke down when she was driving unaccompanied.

The presentation was made at a local pub. The various members of the club had a look at the car in which the radio was to be installed, and agreed that a replacement car would soon be needed. A news reporter was present and a local business man, Robin Coombs, told him that he would approach the Lions club with a view to seeing if they would consider launching an appeal to raise the money to buy a car. Some of the other members did express doubts as to whether such a small group could raise enough, but they thought they ought at least to try.

The next day a report of the presentation appeared in the *Eastern Daily Press*. The story made much of the fact that Angela really needed a new car.

A few days later Mary received a very excited call from Angela.

"Mum, what do you think? I've just had a phone call from a woman who says she wants to buy me a new car. She says she has seen the story in the paper, and it might be a very long time before enough money is raised. She is willing to pay all the cost."

Mary advised caution.

"Don't get too excited, Angi. You know there are some very odd people around these days, and this may be a hoax. Did she give you her name?"

"No, but she sounded pretty genuine to me. Anyway, she asked me all about my disability, and what sort of car would be suitable. I told her I would like a Metro hatchback."

We had discussed at length on a number of previous occasions what car would be satisfactory, and the Metro seemed to fit all the criteria that Angela needed in a car. A hatchback was necessary to accommodate her folding wheelchair, and the Mini was no longer being made.

"Well, Angi, don't build up your hopes too much. Then you

won't be too disappointed if nothing comes of it."

"No, I won't, Mum, but she did say she'd call back to-morrow."

"Well, we'll just have to wait and see then."

Mary found me and reported the substance of the conversation. I was very sceptical too. Who would be generous enough to give nearly six thousand pounds to a stranger on the strength of only a short newspaper report? But perhaps this potential benefactor was not a stranger to us. What if she knew our daughter?

The question of the genuineness of the unknown woman was settled the very next day. Angela and Hartley came to see us, both in a state of high excitement. Our daughter spoke first.

"Mum, Dad, it's true, it's really true. It's happened!"

"What's happened, what's true?" Mary questioned.

"Some woman has actually bought me a new Metro, just like she said on the phone. It's in the Mann Egerton showrooms in Norwich."

"But how do you know this?" I interjected, still half believing that the whole thing was a cruel deception.

"Because she rang me again, this morning, and Hartley rang Mann Egerton to confirm it. The Metro can be picked up at any time. Mum, can you or Dad take me in to get it today?"

"Of course, but I think it would be a wise move for us to ring Mann Egerton again and ask what time would be convenient to call for it," Mary said.

In a very few seconds Mary had confirmed that it would be convenient to pick up the car the very next day.

I don't think any of us slept very well that night, we were all too stimulated by the unexpected turn of events. Two questions still nagged at my mind; was the whole thing a hoax, and who could the woman possibly be?

The first of these questions was answered fully the next day. We arrived at the car showrooms at the appointed time, and sure enough the new Metro was waiting for us, gleaming in the sunlight. We were all as thrilled as was Angela. Again, we asked the salesman to reveal the identity of the benefactor, but he refused to do so. There was a lovely bouquet of flowers for

Angi in the car, and Mary and I spent quite a lot of time look-ing through the big windows to see if there was a lady watching the proceedings. Angela couldn't drive the car right away be-cause there were certain adaptations that had to be carried out by a specialist firm, so Mary had the honour of being the first one to drive it.

After a day or two we were able to arrange for these altera-tions to be made. These included raising the driver's seat, so that Angela would be able to see through the windscreen, ex-tending the brake and accelerator pedals so that she could reach them, and fitting a false floor so that her feet would have something to rest on. After these modifications were done, she could control the car perfectly.

She soon got used to the new car, and I breathed a sigh of relief that she would not have to renew it for at least a few years. Angela took Mary and me for a drive on the first day she was able to drive, and she was so pleased to be able to do so.

The identity of the benefactor continued to elude us. All we wanted to do was to thank her personally, and perhaps let Angela show her how much the car meant. We considered many people that were known to us but we never did get any-where with our deliberations. At length I put a stop to further enquiries. After all, if the woman wanted to be anonymous that was her privilege. We never did find out who had made such a kind gesture. The only way that we ever did get to thank her was by writing to her care of the Mann Egerton salesman, who forwarded our letters. I though she might reply, and therefore reveal her identity, but she did not. After this it was obvious that she really did not want to be discovered and this was almost the end of our search. Later, we had reason to con-tact her again.

After all this excitement and feverish thought we settled down to a normal routine. I think Mary and I refused to acknowledge it at the time, but with hindsight it was clear that Angela's physical condition was deteriorating quite rapidly. There was nothing too specific, nothing too obvious. But her limbs seemed to be stiffer, and she began to get a lot of aches and pains in various parts of her body. The pains which gave us most cause for concern were her frequent headaches. I couldn't bear the thought that she was in pain. She had enough to endure with her restricted movement, without any other difficulty. She also seemed to be subject to bouts of depression.

One Sunday, in our Fellowship meeting, she called out, quite loudly, "I can't go on any longer," crying as she spoke. It was not the first time that this had happened (though not, I think, in the Fellowship), and I went to her to give her some physical comfort. I thought maybe she was just feeling a little sorry for herself. I should have known better, because self pity was not one of Angela's traits. But again my rather off hand dismissal of her problems was because I couldn't bear to face up to the fact that things were going wrong for her. We took her home at the end of the meeting, and she seemed to have recovered her composure. Sometimes, she was not up to driving her car, so Hartley got a provisional licence and drove her. Sometimes he took out the false floor, which made it more or less a normal car, but he was also able to drive it with the floor in place, which I imagine was not strictly legal.

One Monday evening, for example, our two children and their spouses decided to go to the local cinema, involving a journey of about eight miles. Paul had no car at this time and Angela's car was to be used. She did not feel up to driving that night, and so Hartley took the wheel. Paul was a qualified driver, but without removing the false floor he would not fit in to the raised seat. Hartley, being shorter, could.

On the Thursday following this cinema trip, Mary received a phone call from Hartley to tell her that Angela was having a lot of pain in her neck. She had been having a lot of trouble with her neck ever since she had had a spinal examination requiring a myelogram. This had taken place some six months before. On this particular morning the pain was so bad that Hartley had sent for the doctor. On hearing this, Mary rang me at school, and went over to see Angela. She took with her some cream cakes, Angela's favourite form of food. When the doctor had made his examination he said, "I think what she needs is some concentrated physiotherapy, several times each day. It would be most easily arranged if she were admitted to hospital for a few days, say until after the weekend. After some treatment she should be all right again."

Arrangements were made to admit her to the Norfolk and Norwich Hospital in Norwich. Angela didn't like this turn of events. One would have thought that, taking into consideration the number of times she had been in hospitals, she would have got used to it, but she hadn't. But the doctor was insistent. In a short time the ambulance arrived. Mary had some argument with the driver, who wasn't keen to allow Angela to travel in her wheelchair, which was by far the most comfortable for her. But the driver contacted his headquarters and permission was obtained. Mary went home to await my arrival from work.

We arrived at the hospital at 4.30. We found Angela and Hartley in a large waiting room. She didn't look very well. We thought it was quite cold in this room, but Angela complained about feeling hot, and threw off her dressing gown and blanket which we kept putting about her. At about 5.30 Mary found a doctor and asked if a bed could not be found for our daughter. She had been at the hospital for over four hours and was clearly beginning to be distressed, as a result of being kept waiting for so long. Another hour passed, and by now we were all getting rather irate about the situation. Mary could stand it no longer. She found another doctor, explained the situation to him and suggested that a bed be found immediately.

We were getting increasingly concerned about Angela's condition. We had always taken great care that she should never get cold, because with her back and chest deformities a slight chest infection could quickly turn into a life threatening illness. Eventually, a bed was found and the doctor thought it would be advisable to administer some antibiotics. We stayed at the hospital until the staff threw us out at about 9.30. Angela had now settled down and seemed fairly content as we prepared to leave. As we left her, Mary asked, "Have you got any money for the phone?"

"No, but it will be all right. I shan't need to use it."

I thought this was rather odd, as she was always very keen to keep in touch. But perhaps, as she was expecting not to be there for many days, and the fact that Hartley would be in to see her early next morning, she didn't see the need to telephone.

CHAPTER 12

DEATH

After taking Hartley and Paul to their respective homes, Mary and I tried to sleep. We did eventually fall into a rather fitful slumber, after a long read. I seemed to fall into a deeper sleep as the night went on, but I was awakened by Mary's stirring. I became aware that she was using the telephone. Looking at the electronic clock with its big illuminated numbers, I saw that the time was just five minutes past five. In my semi-alert state I wondered who on earth she could be calling at this time in the morning. She surely wouldn't have wanted to wake up Paul or Hartley so early! I just couldn't think of anyone else she could possibly want to contact.

My curiosity was soon satisfied. As she was lying right by my side, I was able to hear both sides of the conversation.

"Hello, is that the Norfolk and Norwich? Could you put me through to Hethersett Ward please? ... Hello, Sister, could you tell me how Angela Graham is please? This is her mother."

Sister's voice crackled down the phone. By now I was fully attentive, my ear pressed close to the outside of the receiver, where I could just about hear the other side of the conversation.

"Well, she's perfectly all right, but what do you think could be the matter?"

"I have been concerned about her all night. I wondered, I feared that she might have got pneumonia."

"I can assure you that she hasn't. I can see her now, and she looks all right to me," came the reply.

Mary's questioning persisted.

"Right, but can you tell me what she's doing right now. Is she sleeping?"

"No, she's not sleeping, she's sitting up in bed reading her Bible."

Before Mary replaced the phone she said, "Thank you, Sister, I'm sorry to have bothered you. Could you tell her that I love her and I'll see her this evening when her dad gets home from work?"

Mary lay back on her pillow, and said, "I'm sorry to have woken you, but I was so worried about her. I'll bet the sister thought I was just another over-anxious mother."

"At least you now know that she's OK," I said, as comfortingly as I could. I, too, thought that Mary was being a bit over-anxious.

We didn't sleep much after that and soon it was time for me to get up for school. I kept thinking that it was strange for Angela to be reading her Bible at that time. She was fond of reading the Bible, but at that early hour? Then I imagined that maybe she found it difficult to sleep in a different place, and so tried to dismiss it from my mind. After all, we would be seeing her in a few hours, and all our doubts and fears would then be resolved.

Mary and I stayed in bed, without sleeping until it was time for me to get up for work. I went into the shower first, and was in the middle of dressing when the phone rang. Thinking it was perhaps one of the school staff ringing up to say they were ill, or something similar, I went to answer it. Mary was still in the bathroom. I was shocked to hear what followed.

"This is Hethersett Ward, Norfolk and Norwich here. Could you please tell me the telephone number of Angela Graham's husband please?"

"Yes, I can. But what's the matter? I am her father."

"Well, Mr Powell, I'm afraid that Angela is not at all well, and I think it would be advisable for her husband to come and see her."

"My wife and I will come as well. If you want I'll let her husband know, but anyway, here is his number."

Mary called in from the bathroom, "Who was that on the telephone, Ed?"

I was still in a state of dumb shock.

"It was the hospital. I think that something is going drastically wrong with Angela. They want us and Hartley to go and see her. She seems to be quite unwell."

Mary started to cry.

"I knew it. I just felt there was something wrong even last night. Right, we'll take Hartley and Paul with us."

Mary called our son and son-in-law, and I rang the school to tell them that I wouldn't be in. I also looked at my list of supply teachers to get someone to cover for me.

Mary and I were downstairs by now, hurrying to get ready for our trip to Norwich. The ring of the telephone interrupted our preparation. Mary rushed to answer it.

Immediately she burst into a paroxysm of crying, screaming and shouting. I could just make out through all the noise, "She's dead. My baby's dead."

She collapsed on the kitchen floor. I removed the phone from her tight grasp.

"What's happened?" I managed to blurt out.

"I'm sorry, but your daughter died a few minutes ago."

"But what went wrong? We rang you round about five o'clock and you said she was all right then."

"She was all right. But her condition deteriorated so quickly. The doctors did all they could, but it was no good. Anyway, you can talk to a doctor when you come in."

I replaced the phone and turned my attention to Mary, who was still on the floor. In a few minutes she was able to sit in a chair, and regained her composure, at least in some small degree.

I rang Hartley just as soon as I was able, but he had already received a message from the hospital. Paul was the next to be informed, and he of course was very upset. He had been a good friend to his sister over the years, and since her marriage he had been the same to her husband. I made arrangements to pick up Hartley and Paul just as soon as Mary and I could get ourselves ready.

I had remained reasonably calm until I realised I would have to call up the school secretary at her home, and ask her to arrange supply cover for me. She had worked at the school for many years, and knew more about the administration than anybody. She knew Angela quite well, as our daughter often used to come to school and help out in the infants' class. She also appreciated how close the members of our family were.

I tried to speak calmly, making a strenuous effort to keep my feelings under tight control. After all, I didn't want one of the "Indians" knowing that the "Chief" couldn't control his emotions.

I started well, giving an impression, I hoped, of complete composure.

"Helen," I began, "I've just heard from the hospital. Angela's dead."

I could hear Helen's sharp intake of breath.

"Oh Eddie, I'm so sorry. . . ."

I interrupted.

"Look, I'm going to have to have some time off."

I couldn't stop myself from crying. It was as if I had used up all my "stiff upper lip" dealing with the events of the past minutes.

"Don't worry at all about the school," I heard Helen say. "I'll get a teacher, and I'll also ring Mr McKeown."

I think she hadn't finished, but I'd had enough and put the phone down. I knew she'd understand my apparent shortness of temper. Malcolm McKeown, the Area Education Officer too would understand too. He had met our daughter on a number of occasions, and admired her courage and tenacity. He would agree to some time off for me.

Although she was a very competent driver, Mary was in no condition to drive, so I drove to Paul's house and then he drove to pick up Hartley and then on to Norwich. There was not much conversation during the journey. My thoughts switched from, "How will Mary cope with life now?" to "Where will she be buried?" I also wondered whether Angela would be in the hospital mortuary by now, or in some special room reserved for the newly dead.

We arrived at the entrance to the hospital car park to find our entrance barred by a "Car Park Full" barrier. There was also a car park attendant on duty. When Paul explained the nature of our visit, he allowed us in to park as members of staff are allowed. We rushed into the building, into the lift and into Hethersett Ward.

None of us had ever been on such a mission. Many questions formed in my mind. Would there be other bodies in the room? Would there be any smell? How would Angela be dressed?

The nurse led us into the ward. I thought we were perhaps going to see a doctor who would be able to tell us the exact circumstances of Angela's death, and maybe advise us on the next procedures. But, instead, we were led to a bed in the middle of the ward. The screens were around the bed.

"She's in there," the young nurse uttered in a very quiet voice. "Are you ready now, or would you like to wait?"

We decided that there was no point in waiting. The sooner the situation was faced the better. I was still hoping that in some way a mistake had been made, and that we would soon discover that the body behind the screen would prove not to be our daughter's.

The nurse opened the curtains a little to allow us to go in. She entered with us, and closed the curtains. We were in a little world of our own.

She was in an ordinary bed, dressed in an ordinary nightgown, with Dopey at her side and her Bible on her pillow. She looked as if she were asleep. I think we all began to weep, but quietly, because we were aware of the sick women only a few feet away, and we didn't want to distress them. We need not have bothered about this though, because obviously they must have been aware of what had happened. I held her hand, and Mary bent to kiss those pale lips. I looked at my watch and calculated that she must have been dead for about ninety minutes, as it was now nine o'clock. We spent some time in complete silence, each lost in his own thoughts.

The voice of the nurse shattered the silence, although she still spoke very quietly.

"Would you like me to get the chaplain to come and pray with you?"

I spoke for the others.

"No, I don't think so. We can manage to pray for ourselves.

But thanks a lot for asking." We didn't stay long. There didn't seem to be much point. I wasn't able to realise it then but we were in a state of shock, and really unable to make any decisions. But before we left, I was able to utter a simple prayer, thanking God for the love that Angela had brought into all our lives. The nurse asked if we wanted any of Angela's possessions. Mary wanted her Bible and watch, but when the nurse started to take off the watch, Mary sobbed, "No, let it stay on."

We emerged from behind the screens, and everybody in the ward seemed to be as children playing statues, perfectly still, watching us. The nurse, who seemed to be in charge of us, led us to a small anteroom and offered us brandy. I was the only one to accept. Hartley had stayed behind for few minutes alone with his wife, and he soon rejoined us. The doctor came in, and asked if we had any questions. Our only query, and the most natural, was, "What was the cause of death?"

The doctor replied, "Of course, we cannot tell for sure before the post mortem, but I'm fairly certain that Angela died because of pneumonia."

"But she was more or less all right when she came into the hospital yesterday. She only came in here for some physiotherapy. How could she have contracted pneumonia in a hospital?" The words cascaded from Mary's lips.

The doctor's face tightened, as if with extreme concentration.

"All I can say at the moment is that pneumonia is my tentative diagnosis, and I am sure this will be confirmed by a post mortem examination. And yes, the illness can come on at great speed, particularly in the case of someone with such physical deformities as Angela. You know, we are all really very sorry."

It was my impression that the expression of regret was genuine.

On the way home Mary was looking at Angela's Bible and found out that on the fly leaf was written,

To our darling Angela, Christmas 1981.
1 Thessalonians chapter 5 verses 16 to 24.

There was not a great deal of conversation. What there was concerned whether there should be a burial or cremation. But this discussion was very brief. I couldn't face the prospect of either, and I guess neither could the others.

We went back to Paul's house, and found the elders of the Cromer Christian Fellowship there to give us the much needed support. In fact we felt the whole membership was supporting us in prayer, which indeed they were. A great comfort too were Paul with his wife, Gill, and children Nicola and Christopher, then aged eleven and nine respectively.

Mary, Hartley and I left and when we arrived at our home, there was a lovely bouquet of flowers. The card read,

From the parents, staff and children –
Blakeney School.

Looking back, I think that Mary and I were in what can only be described as a state of numbness. Otherwise, we could never have borne our grief. It continued for many months, though at the time we were most certainly not aware of it. On that Friday in 1987, it enabled us to cope with the endless stream of visiting well-wishers remarkably well. Most of them said something similar to our local doctor who said: "I know that there is nothing that I can say that will alter the situation, but I just wanted you to know that I am so sorry that this has happened, and I realise what a terrible blow it has been for you."

In some mysterious way, the visitors seemed to bring with them some comfort.

During a lull in the influx of visitors, I took Hartley aside for a conversation that I had been anxious to have with him for several hours. It was now about five o'clock in the evening.

"Hartley," I whispered, "I'd like to have a word with you in private. Come out into the garden for a few minutes."

Once away from all possibility of being overheard, I came to the point.

"I know how upset we all are at the moment, but before long there will be a question that must be considered. Are you going to have Angela buried or cremated."

"To be honest, Eddie, I haven't given it any thought. But I realise that a decision must be made and soon. My first reaction has to be this. Angela is dead, and really I don't see that it makes any difference what happens to her body. I suppose now that I think about it I don't have a preference one way or the other."

This was just the response I wanted to hear.

"If that's the case, do you mind going for cremation? I'll tell you why. If she is buried, it will of course be in a local cemetery, and I'm very much afraid that Mary will spend hours there each day. If it's to be a cremation, then the ashes will be put in the Garden of Remembrance and Mary won't be able to get there so easily. I think that will be by far the better plan, but of course, Mary will realise that the decision is yours. All I'm asking, is that when the question crops up, you say that you want cremation. Is that OK?"

He was crying quietly now, but he managed to nod his assent. I put my arm around his shoulders, and we made our way back indoors to meet some new arrivals.

As soon as the last visitors had gone, I thought it was about time I tackled Mary about the funeral arrangements. Although she didn't really agree with cremation, due to the influence of her father, she had to go along with the wishes of Angela's husband, who, after all, was responsible for the decision. It was not until about three years had passed that I told her of my part in the affair. At the same time she told me how upset she had been over the decision, but certainly at the time I never guessed.

Hartley had agreed that it would be best if he stayed with us for a while, and that night Mary and I made use of the sleeping pills the doctor had left with us. We anticipated we would have trouble in sleeping, but in fact we only used them on a few isolated occasions. I asked Paul to telephone various relatives and friends, and during the evening Mary received a call from our nephew who lives in the United States. He was very sympathetic, and Mary got some much needed strength from his prayers.

We got up early the next day. Although I seemed to have slept well, due to the influence of the tablet, my mind couldn't stop thinking, "I wonder where she is now?"

I asked myself this, not in any spiritual sense, because I firmly believe in the Christian doctrine of the life eternal, but where her body would be. I guess that I really tortured myself by imagining that she would be in a mortuary with a lot of dead bodies, and somehow I just could not really believe that she was dead too.

During the Saturday morning, Hartley and Mary decided that it would be a good thing to go to Hartley's house and sort out Angela's clothes. Gill offered to do this, but Mary felt it was something she had to do. Writing this, some five years later, I cannot imagine how we had the strength. When we arrived at the house which had until so recently been the home of our daughter, we all looked around at the poignant mementoes: a romantic novel lying on the arm of the settee, a sweater in the same area. Most touching of all, in the kitchen amongst the hastily stacked washing up was a half-eaten cream cake which Mary had bought for Angela on the very day she had been taken into hospital. Apparently, the ambulance had arrived before she could finish eating it!

Turning out the wardrobe and drawers was a dreadful task. It seemed that we were getting rid of all vestiges of Angela's very existence. But we persevered. As the garments were very small, there was no one that we could possibly give them to. So they ended up on the local rubbish dump.

There were many people to be telephoned. Angela was known and loved by so many. One of those was our vicar friend, Ian Pusey. He and Ros wanted to come to the funeral, and on hearing this Mary asked him if he'd mind conducting it. This seemed very appropriate, as he had married both our children.

We'd all had enough by the time this was done, and when we had been back at home for about twenty minutes, Deryck, one of the leaders of our Fellowship, came again to see us. He knew we probably wouldn't feel up to attending the Sunday Worship Meeting the next day, he said, but if we could make it he was sure that there would be some help there for us.

Sunday morning saw us in more confusion than ever. Hartley had not attended church for some time, so there was no question of him accompanying us, though we would have wished for this. Eventually, Mary and I decided to go.

The meetings were held in a room at the local Conservative headquarters, on the first floor. As we ascended the stairs, there was complete silence above. I thought this rather odd, as our congregation usually made a lot of noise before the meetings, greeting one another and generally chatting. I imagined that someone had asked them to be quiet as we were likely to attend. But this had not been the case. Perhaps they were all quiet, praying for, and thinking about, the Powell family. Certainly, we felt a sense of sympathy and oneness that we had not really expected, although, of course, we should have, knowing the genuinely loving people that attended, and still do.

Not much of the service is remembered by Mary or myself, but I do recollect that many prayers were said on our behalf. It was not at all easy to take our places in that room, which held so many memories of worship shared with Angela. In fact, in later months, it became quite impossible for us even to enter it.

In my imagination, I could not visualise being strong enough to visit an undertaker's to make the funeral arrangements, but I knew that this would be my task. Maybe I would be too concerned with the actual details, but I would certainly have to be on hand to provide the strength for the rest of the family. And I didn't feel all that strong.

Before his marriage, when he lived in Norwich, Hartley had become friendly with Ian Terry. Ian was a Baptist minister who was then temporarily without a church. He had heard about Angela from Hartley, and he recommended a firm of funeral directors, Peter Taylor of Norwich. He was sure that they would provide the necessary caring service.

So, Monday morning found us in the reception office at Taylor's. We formed quite a party: Paul, Gill, Hartley, Mary and myself. I found one very unusual and important aspect of life during this time. No matter how tragic the circumstance, some humour occasionally comes into the situation. In answer to the various questions in the undertaker's office, it seemed important to all of us that we were unanimous. The question of cremation had already been settled, and in answer to the various other arrangements, I provided a possible answer, and looked to the others for confirmation. I thought that we were like a committee and I couldn't help remarking about this, which raised a little chuckle from several members of the "committee". And, indeed, we did find the staff of Taylor's very helpful and sympathetic, just as Ian had said they would be.

I made one suggestion that I thought might meet with some opposition.

"Just one more thing," I began. "I don't think there's anything to be gained by seeing her again. All of us except Gill have seen Angela, and personally, I would like to remember her as she was then. I think we should ask the undertaker's too, not to allow anyone else to see her."

To my utter astonishment, everyone agreed. My reason for making this suggestion was this. We had seen Angela not long after she had died, and she looked just as if she had been asleep. I thought that it would be very upsetting for me to see her in the artificial, unaccustomed environment of a chapel of rest. While I had been the head of the boarding school at Waltham Abbey I had had to accompany three sets of parents to see their children at these places, and I thought that they were so unnecessarily depressing that I would much rather not see my daughter in such a place. The others apparently had similar ideas too.

Later on the Monday, Mary received a telephone call from Christine, the manageress of the local building society from whom we had obtained our mortgage. Apparently, the society had been running a competition for Mothers' Day, which had been the day before. The competition consisted of writing a letter describing "The Most Wonderful Mother in the World". I imagine that it was really meant for young children, but a number of older people had written in to pay tribute to their mothers, and Angela was one of these. Although she had not won, Christine told Mary that it was a wonderful letter and in view of what had happened, she was sure that Mary would want it. When we read the letter, we realised once more what a wonderful, loving daughter had been lost to us.

90, Woodrow Avenue,
Holt,
Norfolk.
NR25 6TE

20th March 1987

Dear Mrs Townsend,

I should like to nominate my Mum, Mrs Mary Powell, to receive some flowers for Mothers Day.

Let me explain that I am disabled, and although now fairly independent and married, my independence is something I feel was given to me by the sheer love and patience shown to me by my parents.

My mum and I have always been very close, in fact we are so close other people cannot understand our relationship. It is like we are an extension of each other.

As you may imagine, during my early childhood I spent quite a lot of time in hospital, but whenever possible my mum actually came and stayed with me in hospital, and when it was not possible she would visit me every day. For example, when we were living in Staffordshire I was taken seriously ill and eventually ended up in a Liverpool hospital. This was about 70 miles from home. Mum used to telephone the ward at 8 a.m. and she would be walking into the ward at 10 a.m. She did this every day for five weeks.

She is a very loving person both to her children (I have an older brother), to her son and daughter-in-law, to her grandchildren and to everyone in general.

Of course there were times when I was younger that I didn't like the "nagging" to try to do something. However, now that is behind me I see that it was loving encouragement that I was given.

People tell me that despite my disability I am cheerful and friendly. This is not always true as I do have my "off" days like everyone else, but I do believe that to a great extent I owe my personality and ability to do what I can, to my parents.

Please send some flowers to my mum to let her know how much I love and appreciate her and all she has done, is doing and will do in the future.

Thank you very much.

Yours sincerely,

Angi Graham (Mrs)

The funeral was arranged for the following Thursday. The thought of the impending funeral filled Mary and me with dread. I suppose it doesn't really matter what you do with a dead body, but I just could not imagine how I could face up to actually being in the crematorium at the same time as the body of my treasured Angela was being burned up. All right, I wouldn't see the job being done, but I would be in the vicinity. I even contemplated not attending the funeral, but I knew Mary would, and I acknowledged that whatever happened, whatever I felt, I would have to go. But I did not know just how I would cope with it.

As so often happens in such desperate straits, help came from an unexpected source. We talked to our friends, Jeanette and Colin, about the difficulty, and they suggested a meeting with a friend of theirs, Peter Jarrold. Peter is a social worker with the local authority, and has a great deal of experience dealing with people who have emotional problems. Consequently, we arranged a meeting with him on the Wednesday, the day before the funeral.

The meeting with Peter was both traumatic and helpful. He took us through the whole funeral, from beginning to end, frequently asking us about our feelings at each stage. We cried a lot, but honestly, I just don't know how we would have been able to cope with the funeral without his help.

Dopey was something else to be considered. He had been with Angela ever since she was a few weeks old. But, this last time, because of the rush, he had been completely forgotten. We had come across him during our clear out of Angela's clothing. The question now on all of our minds was, "What shall we do with Dopey?"

After much discussion and heartbreak, the family decided that it would be best if he ended his days with Angela. So, he was taken to the undertaker's.

The memories of the day of the funeral are very hazy. I remember sitting down to lunch with Hartley, Ian and Ros. Also something rather wonderful happened, although we did not recognise it at the time. Just as we were leaving for the funeral, Joan, one of our near neighbours, rushed across and put something small in Mary's hand. It was a silver crucifix. Mary and I had never gone in for that sort of decoration, believing that it was a superstitious practice, worn by people who had little faith. Mary put it in her coat pocket (it didn't have a chain), more out of respect for a gift thoughtfully and generously given by a sincere friend than for any other reason. However, as soon as was practicable, we bought a chain, and Mary gained such comfort from it that it has hardly left her neck since. But Mary and I were both in a state of shocked numbness, and my abiding memories consist of staring at the little coffin, and the large number of people present. Ian had suggested that we look at him throughout the service, but somehow my eyes could not keep from moving to the left. I just could not believe that the little body, whom all the family had tried so hard to help, was in the coffin, and beyond all human help. I regret that we did not think to have someone noting the names of those who came. I know this is a common practice, but we did not think of it. It would be so good now to know who exactly were there on that awful day. Seeing the number of people there did, in some way which I cannot at all understand, bring its own little bit of healing. We had arranged with Ian that before the coffin disappeared we would go out. To see it go down out of sight would have been too much. We managed to go through the formalities of shaking hands with all of those present, still in a daze.

When we arrived home, we were amazed to see the wonderful tea that had been put on by members of the Fellowship. It really was marvellous. Also wonderful was the number who had responded to Ian's invitation to come to tea. Again, I now see this as part of the healing process.

I had worn for the funeral the suit bought for Angela and Hartley's wedding, five years before. The day after the funeral, I got out of bed and, thinking about what I should wear that day, I thought I might as well put on the shirt that I had worn for the funeral, as I had had it on for only a few hours. To my horror, I saw that the collar was badly frayed. To think that I had worn this shirt for my daughter's funeral. And I'd shaken hands with all those people. They would have seen it. What would they have thought? I shuddered at the idea. Then, in the midst of the most terrible time of my life, I laughed aloud. How Angela would have been amused to see my consternation at the idea of me being embarrassed over such a small matter!

Hartley stayed with us for the period directly after the funeral. Soon, we had another problem to face. Many months before, we had booked a holiday in southern Spain. It was a package, and we had paid the full cost some two months previously. In view of how we felt, I thought it would be a waste of time going. In fact, it seemed wrong to even think of enjoying ourselves at such a time. So, we took advice. We asked the doctor, the vicar, friends and, it seemed, everyone else. The verdict was unanimous. We ought to go. It would do us good, they said. It was just what we needed, they said. It was the best thing we could do, they said. Also, we felt that we would be letting down Paul's in-laws, Sheila and Alan Nash, who had booked to come with us. We had been friends with them ever since Paul and Gill had first met, and we didn't want to let them down, although of course, in the circumstances, they would have understood. So we went. Hartley was to stay at Paul's house, so we didn't feel too badly about leaving him.

The hotel was first class, and the food excellent. The location was superb, and the weather warm and sunny. We tried our best not to let our own troubles spoil the holiday for Sheila and Alan, but it needed a superhuman effort to do so. One of my holiday treats was to buy a local paper and, with the aid of a Spanish dictionary, try to make sense of the local news. This usually took several days. In this issue, there was a story about a young man who had committed suicide by jumping out of a hotel window on the fourth floor. I was reading this on the balcony of our bedroom. I got up and looked over the parapet, and thought how easy it would be to end all the mental agony that I was suffering. We were six floors up, so if one could be killed from falling four floors, I could be sure to make a good job of it from six.

Suddenly, I was aware that Mary was calling me from the bathroom, and her call made me realise just how foolish and selfish my thoughts of a few seconds ago had been. All right, I had lost my precious Angela, and life would never be the same again, but there were others who needed my help. First, there was my wife. She was finding it probably more difficult to cope than I and what would happen to her if I were gone? Then there was Paul and his family. His daughter, Nicola, was eleven, and Chris only nine. No, doing away with myself would not solve anything. In the whole of my life, that was the only time I have thought of suicide.

During the time in Spain, Mary became very dependent on Paul. At any convenient time she would telephone and seemed to gain a lot of comfort from this contact. It was as if she was frightened of losing him too. Fortunately, he was at home trying to start up his own business, so mostly he was available.

We returned home after our two weeks were up, and Hartley again came to live with us. After a fortnight he began to hanker to return to his own house. We tried gently to dissuade him. We tried to imagine what it would be like for him to sleep in that house without the company of Angela. But he seemed to think that he could cope with it, and so he went back home.

CHAPTER 13

AFTERWARDS

We all tried to be brave during the terrible months that followed. After the Easter holidays I felt that I really ought to get back to school, although I didn't feel at all like facing up to the job. The first day back was very difficult. There I was, surrounded by a number of happy children, each one glad to be back at school, and all raring to get into a new term's work. I couldn't expect them to understand what I was going through, but I got the feeling that some of them did. Certainly, the staff and parents were not slow to show their sympathy. They all knew Angela, who had spent many hours in the infants' classroom. In particular, I was very touched by one little girl, who had just started school. She had, at that time, very severe problems of communication, but on the first day back she crept up behind me and I felt her little hand come into mine. It was if she was saying to me, "Look, I know something of what you are going through, and I want you to know that I am very sorry for what has happened."

All in all, the school helped me enormously. I began to appreciate that I just had to keep on being cheerful. After all, it was not the fault of the children, so I did my best not to be short-tempered with them. The school proved to be a great help to Mary also. On days when she felt particularly down, she would come to work with me. There were always plenty of jobs that she could help out with, and she was greatly helped by being there, amongst all those smiling, happy, eager young faces.

We began to be increasingly worried about Hartley. Not long after the funeral, I made it perfectly clear that Mary and I regarded him as our son, and if he found a girl friend, he was at liberty to bring her to our house, where she would be welcomed. After a while, he joined several dating agencies, but he found no-one special. We did learn that he went out with one girl several times, but his conversation was almost entirely about Angela. He was getting more depressed as the months went by, and he was taking tranquillisers, prescribed by the local doctor. These did help for a short time, but soon he had to be admitted to the local mental hospital. He was there only for a few days, after which he discharged himself. I did not blame him, because it is a most depressing place, and during the time he was there, he appeared to be receiving no treatment at all.

Returning home, he declined our invitation to stay with us, and indeed he seemed to be getting more and more cheerful. On one particular Saturday night, December 12th 1987, we happened to be baby-sitting for Paul and Gill. At about eight o'clock Hartley called in to collect some batteries that Paul had been charging for him. He told us that he was going to a disco, held at the top of the road where we lived. It appeared to Mary and me that he was indeed in very high spirits, and looking forward to the evening out.

The next day, we went to church as usual. The service was about half way through when a familiar face appeared at the door. It was Mike Lord, an ambulance driver whom we knew quite well. He was also a member of the church. He indicated that he wanted to speak to me. Mary and I went out as quietly as we could, wondering what on earth he could possibly want.

When the door was closed, he blurted out, "Hartley's dead – his motor bike."

I knew that Hartley was not the best driver in the world so I assumed that he had met with a road accident.

"What happened? Did he run into something? Was it his own fault?" My questions came so fast that he had no time to answer. When he did get a chance to speak he said quietly, "No, it wasn't a road accident. He committed suicide."

"But how?" I managed to ask.

"Well, he drove his motor bike into his shed, and left the engine running. One of his mates found him about ten o'clock this morning when he called for him."

This news shook us to the very heart of our beings. He had seemed so buoyant only a short time before. What had happened to make him do away with himself? Mike agreed to go into the meeting and tell the others, and we slipped quietly away. We rang the police and found out that Hartley's body had been removed for a post mortem examination, but we could see him if we wanted to.

In the afternoon, we met up with Paul and Gill, and we all decided that we would make all the funeral arrangements after consulting Hartley's father, who was quite prepared to leave it to us. We used the same undertaking firm as we had had for Angela, and we thought it would be appropriate to have the same funeral arrangements as we had had for Angela. The only difference was that Ian Terry, who had been Hartley's best man, conducted the funeral service. Hartley's ashes were scattered amongst Angela's – in plot fifty-four, at the St Faith's Crematorium, Norwich.

CHAPTER 14

RETROSPECT

Writing this, some six years on, I wonder how we coped – how we are coping. Angela was no ordinary daughter. For all of her life she needed help with the most intimate of bodily functions as well as in many other areas, and this necessarily made us feel closer to her than if she had not needed such assistance. Her loss was therefore especially difficult to bear. My object in this chapter is to indicate the particular ways in which Mary and I were helped. Maybe this will help others, either in their own grief, or as guidance in dealing with friends or relatives in theirs.

It is quite wrong to think of ever actually "getting over it". The very concept is quite ridiculous. How can anyone be expected to "get over" the loss of someone who has been loved for so many years? The very idea is farcical in the extreme. But, unfortunately, when one is mourning, even many well-meaning friends expect things to go back to normal after a period of sadness. So, just what did help us?

Above all, it was our Christian faith. We are quite firm and orthodox in our belief, which of course includes an assured hope that what we call death is not the end of everything, but a gateway into a life that is far more glorious than our human minds can ever imagine. We can be glad for them, and we can find great consolation in the certainty that one day we will be reunited with our loved ones. In the meantime, we have to live with the pain of separation from them. We cannot understand why people die when they do, and so we leave the matter entirely in the hands of God, who always knows best. Maybe he took Angela when he did because she had suffered enough. In fact, when I consider the last year or so of her life here, I think it is certain that her physical condition had deteriorated very considerably during this period. But the very thought that this might be happening was so shocking that neither Mary nor I could even consider the possibility for a moment.

We are fortunate that we have a very close and loving relationship with our son and his family. At the time of Angela's death, our grandchildren, Nicola and Chris, were twelve and eight respectively. They and their mother and father were very well aware of the love that Mary and I had for Angela and had a good idea of how deep our grief was. Many times we imposed unmercifully on Paul and Gill's hospitality, frequently into the early hours, but they were always there to listen and sympathise.

Outside the family, the most help we received was from a couple with whom we had made friends a few years previously, Colin and Jeanette. We had got to know them through membership of our church, the Cromer Christian Fellowship. They are about the same age as we are, and for a year or so prior to Angela's death they had been spending every Tuesday evening with us doing some Bible study. They continued to come although Mary and I didn't feel like continuing with the Bible study. Every Tuesday they came, and every Tuesday we would "bend their ears" for several hours, and they never once appeared to find our outpourings at all tedious. This listening very greatly helped us to live with the fact that our daughter was no longer with us.

Again, quite by chance we were put in touch with an organisation, The Compassionate Friends. This group is dedicated to helping people who have lost a child, of any age. We got to know about it through a visitor to a neighbour. We joined and started to attend the local assembly in Norwich. At first, I thought it was a complete waste of time. But after a few meetings I began to realise that by talking to others who had suffered similarly we were able to help each other, mainly by providing "listening ears". I found it helpful to talk to other men, and really open up to them. I got particularly close to one, Peter, whose son, aged twenty-one, had died as a result of a drowning accident. The great thing about these meetings is that nobody is worried if you do have a cry, not even if you are a man!

Help came from a most unexpected source. Ann Jarvis, office manager at the St Faith's Crematorium, has become a very comforting friend. We take flowers to Angi's plot every week, and most times we see Ann. She is never too busy to give us some words of encouragement and we are very grateful to her for this.

It's surprising how difficult our friends found it to say something comforting. Of course, they tried, but it was as though they didn't like to bring up the subject of Angela for fear that the very mention of her name would bring back painful memories. We need no trigger to revive those thoughts: she is in our thoughts most of our waking hours, and sometimes even in our dreams. We love to hear her name being spoken by others. We rejoice when someone recalls some little incident in her life. It gives us great pleasure when we hear a sentence that begins, "Do you remember when Angela . . . ?" Such recollections help us to appreciate all over again what a precious gift Angela was to her family and to so many others.

The following are national contact addresses for the organisations mentioned in this book:

Association for Spina Bifida and Hydrocephalus
Asbah House
42, Park Road
Peterborough
PE1 2UQ

Tel: (0733) 555988

The Compassionate Friends
53, North Street
Bristol
BS3 1EN

Tel: (0272) 539639